THE SHOOTDOWN OF MALAYSIAN FLIGHT 17 AND THE ESCALATING CRISIS IN UKRAINE

JOINT HEARING

BEFORE THE

SUBCOMMITTEE ON EUROPE, EURASIA, AND EMERGING THREATS

AND THE

SUBCOMMITTEE ON TERRORISM, NONPROLIFERATION, AND TRADE

OF THE

COMMITTEE ON FOREIGN AFFAIRS
HOUSE OF REPRESENTATIVES

ONE HUNDRED THIRTEENTH CONGRESS

SECOND SESSION

_____

JULY 29, 2014

_____

Serial No. 113–192

_____

Printed for the use of the Committee on Foreign Affairs

Available via the World Wide Web: http://www.foreignaffairs.house.gov/ or
http://www.gpo.gov/fdsys/

_____

U.S. GOVERNMENT PRINTING OFFICE

88–914PDF   WASHINGTON : 2014

For sale by the Superintendent of Documents, U.S. Government Printing Office
Internet: bookstore.gpo.gov   Phone: toll free (866) 512–1800; DC area (202) 512–1800
Fax: (202) 512–2104   Mail: Stop IDCC, Washington, DC 20402–0001

COMMITTEE ON FOREIGN AFFAIRS

EDWARD R. ROYCE, California, *Chairman*

CHRISTOPHER H. SMITH, New Jersey
ILEANA ROS-LEHTINEN, Florida
DANA ROHRABACHER, California
STEVE CHABOT, Ohio
JOE WILSON, South Carolina
MICHAEL T. McCAUL, Texas
TED POE, Texas
MATT SALMON, Arizona
TOM MARINO, Pennsylvania
JEFF DUNCAN, South Carolina
ADAM KINZINGER, Illinois
MO BROOKS, Alabama
TOM COTTON, Arkansas
PAUL COOK, California
GEORGE HOLDING, North Carolina
RANDY K. WEBER SR., Texas
SCOTT PERRY, Pennsylvania
STEVE STOCKMAN, Texas
RON DeSANTIS, Florida
DOUG COLLINS, Georgia
MARK MEADOWS, North Carolina
TED S. YOHO, Florida
SEAN DUFFY, Wisconsin
CURT CLAWSON, Florida

ELIOT L. ENGEL, New York
ENI F.H. FALEOMAVAEGA, American
Samoa
BRAD SHERMAN, California
GREGORY W. MEEKS, New York
ALBIO SIRES, New Jersey
GERALD E. CONNOLLY, Virginia
THEODORE E. DEUTCH, Florida
BRIAN HIGGINS, New York
KAREN BASS, California
WILLIAM KEATING, Massachusetts
DAVID CICILLINE, Rhode Island
ALAN GRAYSON, Florida
JUAN VARGAS, California
BRADLEY S. SCHNEIDER, Illinois
JOSEPH P. KENNEDY III, Massachusetts
AMI BERA, California
ALAN S. LOWENTHAL, California
GRACE MENG, New York
LOIS FRANKEL, Florida
TULSI GABBARD, Hawaii
JOAQUIN CASTRO, Texas

AMY PORTER, *Chief of Staff*   THOMAS SHEEHY, *Staff Director*
JASON STEINBAUM, *Democratic Staff Director*

(II)

(III)

CONTENTS

THE SHOOTDOWN OF MALAYSIAN FLIGHT 17 AND THE ESCALATING CRISIS IN UKRAINE

TUESDAY, JULY 29, 2014

House of Representatives,
Subcommittee on Europe, Eurasia, and Emerging Threats and
Subcommittee on Terrorism, Nonproliferation, and Trade,
Committee on Foreign Affairs,
Washington, DC.

The subcommittees met, pursuant to notice, at 10:13 a.m., in room 2172, Rayburn House Office Building, Hon. Dana Rohrabacher [chairman of the Subcommittee on Europe, Eurasia, and Emerging Threats] presiding.

Mr. ROHRABACHER. I call this hearing, entitled ''The Shootdown of the Malaysian Flight 17 and the Escalating Crisis in Ukraine,'' to order. Without objection, all members will have 5 legislative days to submit additional written questions or extraneous material for the record.

On July 17th, a civilian airliner flying over Ukraine crashed into a field about 30 miles from the Russian border. All 298 people aboard tragically lost their lives. Today, before we do anything else, let us make it clear that we all extend our sympathy to the families of those victims of that crash. There are 298 families at least who are now in deep mourning and suffering, and they have our sympathy and our thoughts and prayers today.

Our world today seems overwhelmed with such turmoil. On each continent there are various groups battling each other who are willing to use force and kill others in order to change the status quo or to protect the status quo. We see this today, but we also saw this through the 40 years of Cold War that is within our memory. During that time, people in Hungary, Vietnam, Czechoslovakia, and so many other trouble spots were caught up in local differences and local power struggles that had far-reaching, way beyond their borders implications.

Today, Ukraine and Russia are in transition from what is what, and to who knows what is going to happen, but it is a transition, and that transition makes for volatility and undermines the stability, yes, it undermines the stability of the world and threatens world peace.

I intend this hearing today to be a balanced hearing, a dialogue, not a diatribe against any point of view. We have assembled a panel of experts on Russia and the region with a goal of learning the facts and getting a better understanding of the truth; hopefully, without bellicose rhetoric.

Last year, before the upheaval started in Ukraine, Ukraine faced an economic meltdown. Its elected President, Viktor Yanukovych, had a choice between a somewhat long-term yet limited offer by the European Union or a deal with Russia which offered more money up front and long-term affordable energy. He took the Russian deal, not because he was bullied, as some anti-Russian commentators suggest. No, he took the deal because it prevented an immediate crisis and he had every right to make that as the elected leader of Ukraine, and it was a defendable decision.

But because he was duly elected and not a Third World dictator, the Ukrainian people should have used the ballot box to express outrage and remove him from office if that was the will of the majority of the people of Ukraine. Instead, street violence, spontaneous or not is debatable, led to the elected leader fleeing Ukraine, undermining stability, the stability that we are supposed to see that comes with a democracy and comes with people accepting the electoral process.

At the least, it is commendable in the last 6 months, since Yanukovych's removal, the people of Ukraine were given the chance to vote on installing a new President. The ongoing violence in Eastern Ukraine, however, can be traced right back to the violence and extralegal nondemocratic maneuvers of those who brought down that elected President. The ongoing violence is chaotic, and this needs to end. The chaos, the violence, no matter what preceded it, needs to stop now in Ukraine. The MH17 shootdown should be a turning point for all sides. It is time for the guns to stop shooting and some thoughtful reevaluation to commence.

This conflict is having serious, not just regional, but global consequences. For one time over the last few years, Russians and Americans, seem to be headed for a new Cold War. Igniting a new Cold War would be a tragedy for not only the people of the United States and Russia, but for the people of the world. We need to identify and implement policies that will bring the United States and Russia together as partners to solve problems and the serious challenges that we have and the threats that are posed to both of our countries.

Restoring peace to Ukraine would be a good start in deterring a potential new Cold War and establishing perhaps some stability and peace in the world. So today's hearing, hopefully, will identify some of the areas of friction and maybe shed some light on the events in Ukraine that will help permit us to find solutions instead of fanning the flames of conflict.

We have the witnesses who will be introduced just before their testimony, but today we have with us also the ranking member, Mr. Keating, and I would yield to him at this point for an opening statement on his part.

Mr. KEATING. Thank you, Mr. Chairman.

The entire world was sickened by the video footage of so-called separatists sacking the crash site of airline flight 17 over Ukraine on July 17th; almost 300 people losing their lives. And I offer officially my deepest condolences to the families of those victims.

This footage is well-documented, and we have been agonized over reports of bodies decaying in sweltering heat and allegations that separatists continue to disturb and destroy evidence at the crash site. Although the separatists eventually allowed international experts to retrieve most of the victims' bodies and the plane's black boxes, they have continued to prevent international monitors from accessing the crash site. This is completely unacceptable. It is essential that a full and transparent international investigation begin immediately and the fact that this crime must be established and the perpetrators must be brought to justice.

What is most tragic about this disaster is that it was completely avoidable and completely unnecessary. Without prejudging the outcome of a widely hoped-for international investigation, it is entirely accurate to say that this tragedy is the direct result of Russian efforts to sew chaos and instability in Eastern Ukraine and in the wider Eastern European region.

Shockingly, this horrific disaster has not stopped Russia from continuing to fuel the conflict in Ukraine. Russian forces are increasing weapon deliveries to separatists and even firing artillery against Ukraine troops from within Russia. Although it is well within President Putin's power to put an end to this fighting, he continues to insist he has no power over the so-called separatists. Nothing could be further from the truth.

The leaders of the so-called separatists in Eastern Ukraine are not Ukrainian citizens. They are Russian citizens. They are subject to Russian law. Their financing comes from Russia, as do their weapons. Even more troubling, they are trained Russian operatives who fought in Chechnya and worked covertly in Transnistria, Abkhazia, South Ossetia, and even the Balkans to destabilize democratically elected governments, like the current Ukraine Government, and keep them from strengthening ties with anyone but Russia.

I support the administration's use of targeted sanctions in concert with our European allies to press Russia to end its support for so-called separatists in Eastern Ukraine. I am encouraged by the impending agreement by the EU to strengthen sanctions against Russia, and I look forward to the European leaders' decision, which can come as early as today. These measures are designed to show Mr. Putin what the world already knows, that it is well within President Putin's power to end this conflict.

Yes, it is just not our steps or sanctions that are being closely examined, but our commitments to NATO and the transatlantic partnership that continue to be scrutinized by those who are threatening the ideals of rules of law, transparency, accountability, and indeed individual liberties.

For this reason, I urge leaders on both sides of the Atlantic to move forward in setting the global standards for trade, health, environment, and labor by promoting the upcoming TTIP agreement and further would encourage increased dialogue on the future cooperative defense structures under the NATO umbrella as well. These institutions will carry our partnership into the future and offer a window for increased engagements with other like-minded partners throughout the world.

For the immediate future, however, we owe it to the victims of MH17, and to the people of Ukraine, to press Mr. Putin to put an end to his bitter and wholly unnecessary proxy war, a sentiment that has wide agreement on both sides of the aisle in this body.

With that, Mr. Chairman, I yield back.

Mr. ROHRABACHER. Thank you very much.

We are honored today with the presence of the chairman of the full committee, Foreign Affairs Committee, Ed Royce, who we thank you for joining us, and thank you for your leadership in this committee. And we would hope that you might have some thoughts to share with us at this time.

Mr. ROYCE. Thank you very much, Mr. Chairman, and thank you, Mr. Poe. I also want to extend my sympathy to the families who lost loved ones as a result of the downing of that airliner.

I wanted to express my thanks to both of you, and the ranking member, and also to Mr. Poe for coming with us. Frankly, we flew into Eastern Ukraine, into this region, and into the province that is next to Donetsk several months ago in order to have a dialogue with the Russian-speaking people of that region, in order to get feedback from the NGO community, from the community in general. I will tell you we had discussions with Russian speakers, the women's groups, the minority groups, the Jewish community, the governor, the civil society types, the lawyers. And in listening to all of that dialogue, they communicated one grave concern to us. Their concern was in the weapons and the caliber and quantity of those weapons flooding in over the border.

Now, General Breedlove also, who is the Allied Commander at NATO, expressed these same concerns, and this was months ago, and he informed us, he informed the U.S. Government that his concern was with the training that separatists were receiving inside Russia on this SA–11 missile system. His other concern was with these systems, as well as tanks, coming over the border from Russia and being put into the hands of separatists.

Part of the concern about the way this is being done is because of the way in which these separatists are being recruited. They are being recruited on social media. And in the words of one U.S. official, every malcontent and skinhead who responds to this rhetoric in the Russian-speaking world, whether it is from Russia or Eastern Ukraine, who is recruited, is probably not the best soldier. It is not a well-trained soldier, certainly. And to put these types of individuals on an SA–11 system to shoot these systems is to run an enormous risk.

Now, this was a tragic accident in terms of hitting a jetliner, in my view. That was not the target. The target was Ukrainian military planes, and 12 of which had been shot down, and I think several others since. But they are shot down with this system. They are shot down by these individuals. And when we say not properly trained, I don't think there is any question of that, because look for a minute to what happened in front of camera crews when these same separatists were guarding the site, the crash site. You notice that they took passports, they took Visa cards, they tried to use those Visa cards, unprofessional conduct. A soldier would not be doing this. They took someone's wedding ring. They took cell phones and made calls on those cell phones.

This is the concern, this was the type of concern expressed to us by the governor on down in Dnepropetrovsk, the fact that we would have a motley crew like this. And another point they made is that, yes, some speak Ukrainian Russian, but a lot of them are

Muscovites. They speak with a Moscow accent. They are not locals. They are people who have been recruited, been trained, rather poorly trained, and then thrown into this environment.

Our goal has to be to try to wind down this crisis, wind down this situation, and I believe we have an opportunity to do that. We have an opportunity because we have had this election now, and we have a plan which yields a lot of local autonomy. We have a plan which is a rather generous peace plan which, obviously, offers amnesty, as you know, for those who struggled against the government in Ukraine.

You have the will of the local Ukrainian Russian-speaking population, the majority of that population, to be part of this new system because they will be able to elect their own regional representation. But one thing stands in the way. What stands in the way is the insistence on President Vladimir Putin that he continues to bring in heavy weaponry and put that into this struggle, and as a consequence drive up the violence in the region.

Russia is stepping up its actions, and that is why the United States and why Europe is working on a plan now. I must mention, we already passed out of this bill, the Ukraine Support Act, H.R. 4278, we passed this out of committee, myself and Eliot Engel were the authors of it. It expanded our President's authority to increase assistance for democracy and civil society there, and enhanced U.S.-international broadcasting that we are trying to use right now to counter the Russian propaganda in Russia.

The administration has provided $23 million in nonlethal security assistance since March and proposed a $40 million program to train and equip elements of the National Guard in the Ukraine. The announcement yesterday that the U.S. and EU have agreed to impose new sanctions, including on the defense, financial, and energy sectors, is an acknowledgment that the actions taken to date have been insufficient to deter President Putin.

Given that the Europeans can bring far more leverage to bear on Russia than the United States, the responsibility falls heavily on them to convince President Putin that his current course cannot succeed and will only bring increasing pain to his country and his economy. Only under the pressure, that kind of pressure, is he likely to choose peace and finally allow the Ukrainian people to achieve the security, prosperity, and freedom they have so long sought, and I think that is the best course of action. And I yield back.

Mr. ROHRABACHER. Thank you very much, Mr. Chairman.

And we would now like to hear an opening statement from Judge Poe, chairman——

Mr. SHERMAN. Are you going to go Democrat or chairman?

Mr. ROHRABACHER. Okay, Mr. Sherman, the ranking member of the subcommittee.

Mr. SHERMAN. Thank you.

You listen to the American media and it is as simple as an old western movie. That is true of this crisis, that is true of an awful lot of crises where we think that one side is the black hats, the other side is the white hats. This committee, or combination of two subcommittees, has a diversity of views and I think will be a good exposition of the range and complexity of this crisis. I think the one thing we all agree on is that the Time magazine cover, "Cold War II," needs to be avoided.

The plane was shot down, almost certainly with an SA–11 or similar missile, I think certainly an accident, was shot down in a war zone in which separatists were shooting down other planes. The separatists did not use reasonable care to be sure that the plane they were shooting down was, like the other planes they had shot down, a Ukrainian military plane.

There was a lack of care to go around. The Ukrainian Government closed its air space over this area up to 32,000 feet. They knew their own planes were being shot down and it was perhaps the height of arrogance to think, well, they are shooting our planes down at 10,000 or whatever thousand feet, so we will let planes, invite planes to fly over at 32,000 feet.

We have got the Malaysian Airlines aware that planes are being shot down in this zone by not shoulder-fired missiles, but something more advanced, and they said, well, 32,000 sounds good to us, we will go 33,000.

We have got the separatists who clearly didn't exercise due care. And finally, you have a Russian Government who knew better than the Ukrainian Government the military capacities of the separatists and could have closed their own air space along the border, thus making it impossible for civilian planes to fly where civilian planes should not have been flying.

Of course, the separatists could have issued their own, since they style themselves a government, limitation use of the air space. Whether that would have been listened to by anybody, I don't know. But if Russia had closed its air space immediately adjoining this Ukrainian region, planes would have avoided the area.

It is clear that sanctions are justified against Russia. They are interfering in the Ukraine. They are armoring the separatists. And I think that was well summarized by the gentleman from Massachusetts. That being said, our friends in Kiev who want us to take actions on their behalf ought to be taking some actions on their behalf. They ought to be offering the most generous possible package of local autonomy. Instead, they come and say, well, maybe we will continue the practice of having the governors of each oblast—state, if you will—appointed by the central government. I have worked with the gentleman from Texas, and I know if that was the practice here of our Federal Government appointing the Texas governor, well, we might have some problems.

They should be offering budgetary autonomy. They have done so in the vaguest possible words, whereas the Party of Regions, the last party to win an election held in peace, has put forward a more expansive list of actual autonomy. So I am not willing to see the whole world convulsed because those in Kiev could say, well, 51 percent of the people of the entire country support a strict centralized system. It is not our job to work with our allies to get them 100 percent of what they argue is justice. It is our job to work with these allies when there is a great injustice, as we are seeing now.

And finally, there were comments about Yanukovych being driven from power. He ran on a platform, on really a constitutional issue, that he would face west. He then reversed himself and faced east. What I would like to know from the witnesses, because our chairman brought this up, is did the Ukrainian people have a capacity to reverse that reversal through the ballot box or was Yanukovych about to take action which legally was irreversible in signing the agreement with Russia, or as a practical matter would have been irreversible because the EU would not have accepted the Ukraine in its new status after the next regularly scheduled election?

So I look forward to what I think will be a far more wide-ranging and interesting discussion of all of the issues involving the Ukraine and the plane than I have heard in most American media. And I yield back.

Mr. ROHRABACHER. Thank you very much.

And now we have Judge Poe.

Mr. POE. I thank the chairman.

I think it is important that we view this more in a historical long-term perspective than just the isolated, small, tragic issue of the Malaysian airplane being shot down. That is the way I see it.

Putin is the center of all of this. He sees himself as the modern day Peter the Great. Even in a recent profile of Putin, his closest advisors called him czar. Much like Peter the Great, Putin sees and wants an expanding Russian empire.

Any objective observer would conclude nothing has stopped Putin in his desire for more territory. The administration and our European allies have tried to shame and isolate him by kicking Russia out of the G–8. He doesn't care about those diplomatic niceties, and it hasn't had any effect on him or his decision making. Putin and his cronies have brushed off pinprick sanctions and other weak attempts to get him to change his course. He hasn't changed his long-term course, in my opinion. The lack of strong response to Putin's aggression has only really encouraged him to be more aggressive.

And then over the sky of Eastern Ukraine, a surface-to-air missile was launched and it destroyed the Malaysian civilian airliner. This dastardly deed killed—rather murdered—298 people. The missile and launcher were Russian. This is a photograph of a similar missile launcher that is Russian made. The individuals shooting down the plane were so-called Russian-backed separatists in Ukraine, and apparently the crash site, which is a crime scene on the ground, is controlled by pro-Russian sympathizers, and it has been compromised by malcontents. As the chairman pointed out, they are pillaging the wreckage site, taking property from the people that were murdered on that plane. Unlike the civilized world, Putin's reaction was to deny that he had anything to do with it and persist in outlandish Area 51-type conspiracies about who did it.

Putin, I call him the Napoleon of Siberia, has fingerprints all over this Lusitania-type incident. This is the latest in a series of aggressive acts by the Russian bear. I did mention in this committee on March 25th that Putin is determined to start Cold War II. Ever since then, he keeps doing things to encourage that philosophy of wanting to be starting that Cold War II again.

In 2008, years ago, most Americans don't even remember, the Russians invaded the sovereign nation of Georgia. Not the State of Georgia, but the nation of Georgia—unlike one of our fellow committee members—was worried about Georgia being invaded and he missed it. It was the Republic of Georgia. The Russian bear gobbled up one-third of the territory. The world leaders, they protested loudly, but they were glad it wasn't their homeland, and then the world moved on. The Russian tanks are still in one-third of Georgia. I have seen them. I have been there.

Then the Russian bear hibernated for a while and then in 2013 it woke up hungry and it had its sights on its prey of Crimea. That belongs, still belongs, to Ukraine. So to satisfy its appetite for more czar-like territory it was gobbled up. Now the Russians unlawfully occupy Crimea. The world leaders once again got on television and voiced opposition, then they went off back to their policy of what I call appeasement.

So, still hungry, the bear of the north woke up again in Eastern Ukraine, looked for more prey, and it subversively has supported insurrection against the Ukrainian Government to gain more territory. Reports indicate Russian special forces are playing the role of pro-Russian separatists, Russian special forces that were similarly pretending to be Georgian separatists. Battles are being fought, people are dying, and Russian imperialism persists in its aggression. This seems like this is a war to me on Ukraine.

And then the Malaysian airplane was shot down. Also, as the chairman pointed out, other Ukrainian military aircraft have been shot down. Two Ukrainian military jets, over Ukrainian sovereignty, were shot down by Russian missiles fired from Russia. That seems to be somewhat aggressive. The world leaders are outraged, but the bear has not stopped.

So what will the heads of states do? Will the world leaders continue to take the position the bear hasn't eaten them and they will do little but pontificate and hope the bear's appetite is satisfied? Maybe the bear will hibernate again. When it wakes up, like it always has, it will wake up hungry, and then when it roars, who will be devoured next, the rest of Ukraine, Moldova, Latvia, Estonia, Poland, or just another group of people on an airplane flying over another country? Only Putin knows what the roar of the Russian bear will bring to the rest of us.

Appeasement certainly doesn't seem to be working, doesn't seemed to have stopped the aggression. It is important that we do what we can to help the Ukrainian nation keep its sovereignty. Yes, it is their country. They should defend it. It is their responsibility. But we can provide them military equipment, jam Russian missiles. The Russians must be made to understand they have to stop invading other people's territory.

Second, as when I was in Ukraine, all the Ukrainians talked about was being energy independent from Russia. That is, developing their own natural gas to compete against Gazprom and getting U.S. natural gas to them. They wanted that. They don't know our answer on that.

And third, we actually need sanctions that work to have an impact. So I ask the question: Is there not one bold Churchill to be found among the overpopulated, boastful Chamberlains among the world leaders? We shall see.

I yield back.

Mr. KEATING. Will the gentleman yield? Will the gentleman yield?

Mr. POE. I yield back.

Mr. ROHRABACHER. We will have some time for interaction after the witnesses testify. And I guess, Your Honor, that is just the way it is.

We are going to go to the witnesses now. And anyone who has an opening statement, or extraneous material to add to the record at this point, it will be added to the record, without objection.

We have four witnesses with us today. I would ask if they could try to, unlike the rest of us up here, limit the actual testimony to 5 minutes, although your written testimony can be as long as you would like. And then we will actually try to have a dialogue on this and ask you about the positions you have taken, and perhaps some questions that will utilize your expertise and help us get a better understanding of exactly what is going on in Ukraine.

I will introduce all four witnesses and then we will proceed with the testimony of each witness, and then a question-and-answer period.

Our first witness is Ian Brzezinski, a senior resident fellow with the Brent Scowcroft Center on International Security at the Atlantic Council. He served as deputy assistant secretary of defense for Europe and NATO policy between 2001 and 2005. He has a long tenure of working with national security issues, including working on Capitol Hill for 7 years. He also worked as a volunteer in Ukraine in the early 1990s, advising the Ukrainian National Security Council, Foreign Ministry, Defense Ministry, and Parliament.

We have Anthony Salvia, who is the director of the American Institute in Ukraine, a privately funded, nonprofit organization dedicated to providing information and education about the United States policy in that country. He served as an executive assistant to the president of Radio Free Europe, Radio Liberty from 1988 to 1993, and then went to Russia as director of the Moscow Programming Center for the RFE–R, Radio Free Europe/Radio Liberty, from 1993 to 1996. He is a graduate of Johns Hopkins University, has a master's degree in European Affairs and International Economics.

Next we have Dr. Leon Aron. He is a resident scholar and director of Russian studies at the American Enterprise Institute here in Washington. He is widely published. He is an expert on Russia, having authored three books and hundreds of articles on the subject. He is also a frequent media commentator, and earned both a master's degree and his Ph.D. From Columbia University.

And we have with us Ambassador William Taylor. He is the vice president for Middle East and Africa at the U.S. Institute of Peace. From 2011 to 2013, he was the special coordinator for the Middle East transitions at the Department of State, and he has also coordinated our assistance to Egypt Tunisia, Libya, and Syria. He served as the U.S. Ambassador to Ukraine from 2006 to 2009. Before that, he served in Baghdad and Kabul. He is a graduate of West Point and a veteran of the United States Army.

We turn to our witnesses now. And, Mr. Brzezinski, you may proceed.

STATEMENT OF MR. IAN BRZEZINSKI, RESIDENT SENIOR FELLOW, BRENT SCOWCROFT CENTER ON INTERNATIONAL SECURITY, ATLANTIC COUNCIL

Mr. BRZEZINSKI. Chairman Rohrabacher, Chairman Poe, Ranking Member Keating, Ranking Member Sherman, members of the committee, thank you for the privilege of appearing before this hearing to discuss ramifications of the shootdown of Malaysian Airlines flight 17. That tragedy is the consequence of Russia's invasion of Ukraine, and specifically the Kremlin's stoking of an insurrection in Eastern Ukraine. The MH–17 shootdown should prompt us to carefully assess the effectiveness of the West's response to these provocative acts of aggression.

The invasion of Ukraine began in February. Today, some 6 months later, Russia still occupies Crimea. The insurrection in Eastern Ukraine, which has intensified, has been led and fought by Russian operatives, enabled by Russian weapons, and reinforced by Russian military forces massed along Ukraine's border.

Yesterday the United States and West European officials announced agreement on a new set of sanctions against Russia. As we learn more about these sanctions, I hope they will mark a departure from the empty warnings, brooding ministerials, and the hesitancy and incrementalism that has characterized the West's reaction to this invasion.

Indeed, over the last 6 months, U.S. policy appears to have been shaped more by the lowest common denominator of what our allies are willing to do rather than by initiative and decisive action on the part of Washington. And it has been counterproductive. It has emboldened Russia. After each increment of targeted sanctions, Russia has increased its support to its proxies in Ukraine. The Kremlin's deployment of irregulars with small arms is now complemented by training and recruitment centers in Russia, and its transfer to its proxies of tanks, rocket launchers, surface-to-air missiles, including most notably the Buk SA–11 air defense system, among other equipment.

If the pending decisions by the United States and the EU are a continuation of past hesitancy and incrementalism, they risk leading to a stalemate in Ukraine, another frozen conflict that will leave Ukraine crippled and unable to pursue its European aspirations. Worse, it can embolden Putin to press further into Ukraine and pursue similar strategies toward Moldova and the Baltic States.

The West needs a comprehensive strategy, targeted at persuading Putin to remove his forces from Ukraine, deterring Russia from further aggression against Ukraine and other neighboring countries, reinforcing Ukraine's capabilities for self-defense and assisting Ukraine to become a prosperous, democratic European state.

Towards these ends, the U.S. should undertake the following initiatives. First, stronger economic sanctions against Russia are in order. The overly selective scope of current sanctions has failed to inflict the systemic economic pain necessary to make an authoritarian regime rethink its actions. Sectoral sanctions should be imposed and the key targets should be Russia's energy and financial sectors. There should be no loopholes and no exceptions.

Second, a more robust effort is needed to shore up NATO allies in Ukraine. In early June, President Obama announced the European Reassurance Initiative to reinforce Central European allies and build the military capabilities of East European partners. This is an important initiative, but almost 2 months later it remains unclear exactly what it will yield. It would be useful if the ERI established a strategically significant U.S. enduring military presence in Poland and the Baltic States. It would be even better and more useful if NATO's West European allies contributed to this initiative.

Third, we need to provide military assurance to Ukraine. To date, NATO and the United States have unwisely done the opposite. They have drawn a red line on the alliance's eastern frontier that leaves Kiev militarily temporarily isolated. Now that Russia is firing artillery into Ukraine, erasing that red line has become more urgent.

Toward that end, the United States should grant Ukraine's request for lethal military equipment, including surface-to-air missiles and anti-tank weapons, deploy intelligence and surveillance capabilities in Ukraine, along with military trainers, conduct military exercises in Ukraine to help train its armed forces. None of these initiatives would threaten Russian territory.

Fourth, the West needs to step up its efforts to counter Russia's aggressive propaganda campaigns. The Kremlin's effort against Ukraine in this realm has been the most intense we have seen since the end of the Cold War.

Fifth, the West needs to support Ukraine's effort to reform its economy and integrate into Europe. To its credit, Washington has done well in mobilizing international financial support for Ukraine. Freeing up U.S. LNG exports to Central and Eastern Europe would be another way to reinforce the region's security and help Ukraine diversify its energy base.

And finally, the West needs to reanimate the vision of a Europe whole, free, and secure. The situation in Eastern Europe today necessitates that NATO make clear its open-door policy is no passive phrase or empty slogan.

Mr. Chairman, the shootdown of MH–17 is a stark reminder of how regional conflict can have immediate implications far beyond its immediate vicinity. I hope the sanctions that are being rolled out today will reflect a firmer response and stronger leadership on the part of the United States. That will be necessary if the West is going to convince President Putin to reverse his dangerous course.

Thank you.

[The prepared statement of Mr. Brzezinski follows:]

The Shoot Down of Malaysian Flight 17 and the Escalating Crisis in Ukraine

A Joint Subcommittee Hearing
Subcommittee on Europe, Eurasia and Emerging Threats
Subcommittee on Terrorism, Nonproliferation, and Trade

29 July 2014

Submitted Testimony
by
Ian J. Brzezinski,
Resident Senior Fellow, Brent Scowcroft Center on International Security
Atlantic Council

Chairman Rohrabacher, Chairman Poe, Representative Keating, Representative Sherman, thank for you for the privilege of appearing before the committee to discuss the ramifications of the shoot-down of Malaysian Airlines Flight 17.

That tragedy is the consequence of Russia's invasion of Ukraine and specifically the Kremlin's stoking of an insurrection in eastern Ukraine. The MH17 shoot-down should prompt us to carefully assess the effectiveness of the West's response to these provocative acts of aggression.

The invasion of Ukraine began in February. Today, some six months later, Russia still occupies Crimea. The insurrection in eastern Ukraine, which has intensified, has been led and fought by Russian operatives, enabled by Russian weapons, and reinforced by the deployment of Russian military forces along Ukrainian border. Recently, artillery based in Russia fired across that border at Ukrainian forces.

This invasion is an affront to the principles that have kept in peace in Europe, including respect for territorial sovereignty and the right of states to freely pursue their own affiliations uninhibited by the threat and exercise of force. President Putin's assertion that he has the unilateral right to redraw borders to protect ethnic Russians reintroduces a dangerous principle that in past centuries has provoked wars and caused countless deaths in Europe.

The invasion of Ukraine is but one element of a sustained revanchist policy that Vladimir Putin has articulated and exercised as president of Russia. His objective has been to reestablish Russian hegemony, if not full control, over the space of the former Soviet Union. Toward this end, he has applied the full suite of Russian economic, energy, political, and military capacities to weaken and dominate neighboring states. He has leveraged information and cyber warfare, corruption and criminal networks, political provocateurs, separatist groups, frozen conflicts, and military incursions, among other means. His campaign history includes the 2007 cyber attack against Estonia, the separatist movement in Moldova, energy embargoes against Lithuania and Ukraine, and the 2008 invasion of Georgia.

To date, the West's response to Putin's invasion of Ukraine has been underwhelming. It is characterized by stern warnings, brooding ministerials, and hesitant, incremental actions on both the military and economic fronts.

US policy appears to be shaped more by the lowest common denominator of our what our allies are willing to do rather than by initiative and decisive action on the part of Washington. This is "leading from behind," and as a result the West is far from leveraging the full capacities of its economic, political and military power.

In fact, it has been counterproductive. After each increment of targeted sanctions, Russia has increased its support to its proxies in Ukraine. The Kremlin's deployment of irregulars with small arms is now complemented by its training and recruitment centers in Russia and its transfer to these ill-disciplined militias of tanks, rocket launchers, shoulder-launched surface-to air-missiles, and other equipment, including most notably, the Buk SA-11 air defense system.

Rhetoric alone will not change President Putin's calculus. In the absence of greater resolve from the West, he will continue to drive forward to further implement his vision. The West's current posture risks a stalemate in Ukraine, another frozen conflict that will leave Ukraine crippled and unable to pursue its European aspirations. Worse, it could emboldened Putin to press further into Ukraine and pursue similar strategies toward Moldova and the Baltic States.

The West needs a strategy targeted toward these four objectives:

- Persuading President Putin to remove his forces and proxies from Ukraine;
- Deterring Russia from further aggression against Ukraine and other neighboring countries;
- Reinforcing the capacity for self-defense of Ukraine and other democracies along Russia's periphery; and,
- Assisting Ukraine's effort to become a modern, prosperous democratic European state.

Toward these ends the US should undertake the following initiatives:

First, stronger economic sanctions against Russia are in order. The overly selective scope of current sanctions has failed to inflict the systemic economic pain necessary to make President Putin's authoritarian regime rethink its actions. Sectoral economic sanctions should be imposed, and the key targets should be Russia's energy and financial sectors.

We should not underestimate the economic leverage that two globally integrated economies -- the $12 trillion EU economy and the $16 trillion US economy -- can exercise against Russia's frail $2 trillion dollar economy, one whose primary source of revenues is the sale of gas to primarily one customer, the European Union.

Second, the West's economic and diplomatic sanctions need to be complemented by a robust strategy to shore up NATO allies and Ukraine.

NATO's response to the invasion of Ukraine has been limited to a largely symbolic reinforcement of NATO air space, the rotation of a ship to the Black Sea, and some special forces and army companies to Central Europe. This is sharp contrast to the nearly 100,000 troops Russia mobilized on its western frontier when it commenced its invasion of Ukraine.

In early June, in Warsaw, President Obama announced the European Reassurance Initiative (ERI) to reinforce Central European allies and assist East European partner states strengthen their militaries. This is an important initiative with great potential, but two months later it still remains unclear exactly what it will yield. It would be useful if the ERI would yield a strategically significant US enduring presence in Poland and the Baltic States to complement US forward operating bases in Romania and Bulgaria. It would be even more useful if NATO's West European Allies contributed to this initiative.

These steps would help generate a context of security and confidence to Ukraine's immediate west.

Third, we need to provide military assurance to Ukraine: To date, NATO and the United States have done the opposite. They have drawn a red line on the Alliance's eastern frontier that leaves Kyiv militarily isolated. Now that Russia has fired artillery into Ukraine, erasing this red line has become more urgent.

Toward that end, the United States should:

- Grant Ukraine's request for lethal military equipment and include anti-tank and anti-aircraft weapons. U.S. equipment, in particular, would reawaken in Moscow unpleasant memories of when Soviet forces last encountered them in Afghanistan.

- Deploy intelligence and surveillance capabilities and military trainers to Ukraine. This would force Moscow to consider the repercussions of any actions it takes affecting that presence. The U.S. deployment of military trainers to Georgia after it was invaded by Russia contributed usefully to that country's security.

- Conduct military exercises in Ukraine to help train its military. The indefinite postponement of EUCOM's RAPID TRIDENT exercise in Ukraine this summer can only have been interpreted by the Kremlin as a sign of weakness and possibly emboldened it to step up its military action Eastern Ukraine.

None of these initiatives would threaten Russian territory. They would, however, introduce uncertainty into Moscow's planning regarding Ukraine, and force it to consider the risks of a costly and prolonged military conflict.

Fourth, the West needs to counter Russia's aggressive propaganda campaigns. The Kremlin's information operation against Ukraine has been the most intense we have seen since the end of the Cold War. It weakens the political unity required for Ukraine to undertake necessary and painful economic reforms. It creates opportunity for the provocateurs Moscow has sent into the country. Similar information campaigns cloud public perceptions among Russia's other neighbors.

Fifth, the West needs to support Ukraine's effort to reform its economy and integrate into Europe: To its credit, Washington has done well in mobilizing international financial support for Ukraine.

One area where more can be done is the diversification of Ukraine's energy supplies and its integration into the European energy market. Freeing up U.S. LNG exports to Central and Eastern Europe would serve this priority. This over the long term would dilute Moscow's excessive leverage in their gas markets, but in the near and middle term it would help drive forward necessary investment and transmit a powerful signal of transatlantic solidarity.

Finally, the West needs to reanimate the vision of a Europe whole, free and secure. The situation in Eastern Europe today necessitates that NATO make clear its "open door policy" is no passive phrase or empty slogan.

Reaffirmation of this vision is an important way to underscore Washington's commitment to the security of Central Europe. The NATO Summit in Wales this September provides another high-profile opportunity to bring life back to the process of NATO enlargement through the extension of an invitation to Montenegro or the Alliance's membership action plan to Georgia.

The most effective way to counter President's Putin's hegemonic aspirations is to deny them opportunity for actualization. The presence of secure and prosperous democracies in Russia's neighborhood is not threatening but it can help redirect Moscow's focus toward its pressing internal problems. It may even provide momentum to those Russians who have grown weary of authoritarianism, corruption and antiquated notions of empire.

Security in Central and Eastern Europe has always been essential to the forging of a true and enduring partnership between Europe and Russia, and between Washington and Moscow.

———————

Mr. ROHRABACHER. Mr. Salvia.

STATEMENT OF MR. ANTHONY SALVIA, EXECUTIVE DIRECTOR, AMERICAN INSTITUTE IN UKRAINE

Mr. SALVIA. Thank you, Mr. Chairman. And thank you to Judge Poe and Congressman Keating and Congressman Sherman and the whole committee for the opportunity to address this joint sub-committee of the House Foreign Affairs Committee.

The controversy over the shootdown of Malaysian Airlines flight 17 remains unresolved. There are the predictable charges and countercharges, which are no substitute for proper investigation resulting in the conclusion that all parties, above all Russia and Ukraine, can and must accept.

Meanwhile, the conflict in Eastern Ukraine continues to grind on to the detriment of all Ukrainians. It is safe to say many hundreds have died. I think the New York Times said yesterday 800 since April have died in Eastern Ukraine and thousands have been wounded. According to the U.N., some 230,000 have fled their homes, of whom more than 100,000 have been driven out of the country. Donetsk, a city of 1 million, is under siege. Its water supply is at risk. Sections of the city have no electricity, sewage, or gas. Shops are closed. Food is increasingly hard to come by.

What will happen now? Will there be a cease-fire leading to a negotiated settlement so as to salvage Ukraine's increasingly slim prospects for unity? Or will Kiev continue to seek a military victory in the east and use the National Guard, which includes in its ranks member of the extreme nationalist Praviy Sektor, to repress the native population?

As of now, Kiev seems determined to prosecute the war, which means in the context to create demographic change in the country. Kiev cannot afford to pay its soldiers. There is a high rate of desertion and Ukraine's economy is teetering on the brink of collapse. But it is making headway in one area, namely in the killing of East Ukrainian civilians, which Western observers at long last have begun to take note, including a New York Times article of yesterday.

And indeed, as Human Rights Watch reported last week from Donetsk,

> ''Unguided rockets launched apparently by Ukrainian Government forces and pro-government militias have killed at least 16 civilians and wounded many more in insurgent-controlled areas of Donetsk and its suburbs, in at least four attacks between July 12 and 21, 2014. The use of indiscriminate rockets in populated areas violates international humanitarian law, or the laws of war, and may amount to war crimes.''

Nevertheless, there is no evidence that Kiev is curtailing the use of these missiles in populated areas or, for that matter, the resort to air power and artillery against anti-Kiev fighters Poroshenko calls terrorists, dirt, and parasites. Poroshenko brushed off calls from Paris, Berlin, and Moscow to extend his June 20th cease-fire and resumed his offensive against his own people. The Eastern

Ukrainians are responding by shooting down as many of Kiev's military plans as they can and the cycle of violence spins on.

There are those in Washington who see Ukraine not at all for itself, but strictly as an adjunct to its obsession with Russia, concerning which the prevailing attitude is, we must win, you must lose. Perhaps Washington and its friends in Kiev can succeed in decimating Donetsk and Luhansk, but this is not likely to be the end of it.

Indeed, in the Washington Post just the other day, I believe it was the day before yesterday, Serhiy Kudelia of Baylor University wrote about the prospect of you can defeat Donetsk and Luhansk, but what about a long-term counterinsurgency that leaves the place in a state of not the same degree of upheaval as all-out war, but a situation of a lack of resolution, a kind of Northern Ireland situation, only worse.

It is unlikely Poroshenko would be embarked on his present course without Washington's support and pressure from his own radical nationalists. It is telling that on July 22nd, President Obama called for a cease-fire in Gaza, but said nothing about a cease-fire in Ukraine.

There is no military solution to Ukraine's internal problems, which are political, economic, and cultural in nature. Ukraine is the second-poorest country in Europe. Its foreign exchange reserves are shot. All resources are being poured into the campaign to destroy the most prosperous part of the country, East Ukraine.

And indeed, Serhiy Kudelia, writing in the Washington Post the day before yesterday, I don't know how he came up with this figure, but he put a figure of $800 million on the need just to conclude this campaign on the part of the Kiev government. Where are they supposed to get this money when they are in arrears to the tune of multi-, multi-, multi-millions and billion, and then to add on this expense? Where does the money come from?

As former Acting Prime Minister Yatseniuk stated upon his recent resignation, the coalition, the governing "coalition of Fatherland, UDAR, and Svoboda has fallen apart. Laws haven't been voted on. Soldiers can't be paid. There is no money to buy rifles. There is no possibility to store gas. What options do we have?" asked Yatseniuk.

Well, there is this option: A comprehensive cease-fire, genuine negotiations, and a balanced settlement that addresses Ukraine's real needs. Such an approach would command wide European and especially German support.

Dr. Robert Legvold of Columbia University in New York recently observed that Europeans will not support one side pushing for military victory over the other. He said,

> "Kiev's part in the political dialogue must be flexible and genuinely open to meeting the concerns of the majorities in all of Ukraine's eight eastern provinces. It means more than convening peace talks, even if without preconditions. It means getting the U.S., the United States, to invest more effort in drawing all parties toward a political settlement."

That is the heart of the matter, how do we get Washington on board with the idea of a cease-fire negotiation, a peaceful settlement? Thank you.

Mr. ROHRABACHER. Thank you very much.

[The prepared statement of Mr. Salvia follows:]

Anthony T. Salvia

Testimony before the Joint Subcommittee of the Europe, Eurasia and Emerging Threats Subcommittee and the Terrorism, Non-Proliferation and Trade Subcommittee of the House Foreign Affairs Committee

July 29, 2014

Dear Mr. Chairman,

Thank you for having invited me to testify before this distinguished Joint Subcommittee of the House Foreign Affairs Committee. It is truly a great honor.

I have been involved professionally for more than 30 years with Central and Eastern Europe, including the ex-USSR – first as an appointee of President Ronald Reagan to the Departments of Defense and State, then as executive assistant to the President of Radio Free Europe/Radio Liberty, where, living in Germany, I experienced at close range the momentous events surrounding the collapse of the Berlin Wall, then, as the chief of RFE/RL's Moscow bureau during the Yeltsin years, in which capacity I was able to observe the ups and downs of Russia's efforts to overcome 70 years of Communist misrule. In recent years I have been active with the American Institute in Ukraine -- a privately funded U.S. nonprofit organization that provides information, education and analysis on U.S. policy towards Ukraine, and seeks to reflect the diversity of US opinion in this area.

In that capacity, I have been in Ukraine a dozen times in the past five years, although I first visited the country in 1991 – shortly after the dissolution of the USSR.

The controversy over the shoot-down of Malaysian Airlines flight 17 remains unresolved though it is no longer at fever pitch. The predictable charges and counter-charges are no substitute for a proper investigation, resulting in a conclusion that all parties, above all, Russia and Ukraine, can and must accept.

Meanwhile, the conflict in Eastern Ukraine continues to grind on to the detriment of all Ukrainians. It is safe to say many hundreds have died, and thousands have been wounded. According to the UN, some 230,000 have fled their homes of whom more than 100,000 have been driven out of the country. Donetsk, a city of one million, is under siege; its water supply is at risk. Sections of the city have no electricity, sewage, or gas. Shops are closed; food is increasingly hard to come by.

What will happen now? Will there be a cease fire leading to a negotiated settlement so as to salvage Ukraine's increasingly slim prospects for unity?

Or will Kiev continue to seek a military victory in the east, and use the National Guard, which includes in its ranks members of the extreme nationalist *Praviy Sektor* (often referred to as neo-Nazi), to repress the native population?

As of now, Kiev seems determined to prosecute the war – which means, in the context, to cleanse the east ethnically of people it has no use for. Kiev cannot afford to pay its soldiers, there is a high rate of desertion, and Ukraine's economy is teetering on the brink of collapse. But it *is* making headway in one area -- namely, in the killing of East Ukrainian civilians, of which Western observers, at long last, have begun to take note. As Human Rights Watch reported last week from Donetsk ["Ukraine: Unguided Rockets Killing Civilians: Stop Use of Grads in Populated Areas"]:

> Unguided Grad rockets launched apparently by Ukrainian government forces and pro-government militias have killed at least 16 civilians and wounded many more in insurgent-controlled areas of Donetsk and its suburbs in at least four attacks between July 12 and 21, 2014. The use of indiscriminate rockets in populated areas violates international humanitarian law, or the laws of war, and may amount to war crimes. [...] Grad rockets are notoriously imprecise weapons that shouldn't be used in populated areas," said Ole Solvang, senior emergencies researcher at Human Rights Watch. "If insurgent and Ukrainian government forces are serious about limiting harm to civilians, they should both immediately stop using these weapons in populated areas."

Indeed they should, but there is no evidence Kiev is curtailing the use of these missiles in populated areas, or, for that matter, the resort to air power and artillery against anti-Kiev fighters Poroshenko calls "terrorists," "dirt" and "parasites." Poroshenko brushed off calls from Paris, Berlin and

Moscow to extend his June 20th ceasefire, and resumed his offensive against his own people. The Eastern Ukrainians are responding by shooting down as many of Kiev's military planes as they can, and the cycle of violence spins on.

A piece in the *New York Times* of last Sunday (July 27,2014) does not bode well for the cause of peace and reconciliation in Ukraine. It reports the Pentagon is considering developing a plan to help Ukraine locate the surface-to-air missile batteries of the anti-Kiev partisans. This will have the effect of facilitating Kiev's ability to terrorize and decimate the civilian populations of Donetsk and Lugansk by leaving them unprotected against strikes from the air.

There are those in Washington who see Ukraine not at all for itself, but strictly as an adjunct to its obsession with Russia, concerning which the prevailing attitude is "we must win, you must lose." Perhaps Washington and its friends in Kiev can succeed in decimating Donetsk and Lugansk, but that is not likely to be the end of it.

Writing last week in the *Washington Post*, Baylor University's Serhiy Kudelia sees Kiev's bellicosity as opening the door to a long-term counterinsurgency. He notes Kiev's need for $800,000,000 to finish off the enemy (where is that supposed to come from?), and says Poroshenko – far from meeting the partisans' demand for greater regional autonomy -- has actually introduced legislation that would give him veto power over local decision-making.

It is unlikely Poroshenko would be embarked on his present course without Washington's support and pressure from his own radical nationalists. It is telling that on July 22, President Obama called for a ceasefire in Gaza, but said nothing about a ceasefire in Ukraine.

There is no military solution to Ukraine's internal problems, which are political and economic in nature. Ukraine is the second poorest country in Europe. Its foreign exchange reserves are shot. All resources are being poured into the campaign to destroy the most prosperous part of the country – East Ukraine. As former Acting Prime Minister Arseniy Yatseniuk stated upon his recent resignation:

"The coalition [of Fatherland, UDAR and Svoboda] has fallen apart, laws haven't been voted on, soldiers can't be paid, there's no money to buy rifles, there's no possibility to store up gas. What options do we have now?", *asked Yatseniuk.*

Well, there is this option: a comprehensive ceasefire, genuine negotiations, and a balanced settlement that addresses Ukraine's real needs. Such an approach would command wide European – and especially German support.

Dr. Robert Legvold of the Columbia University in New York recently observed that Europeans will not support one side pushing for military victory over the other. He said:

> "Kyiv's part in a political dialogue must be flexible and genuinely open to meeting the concerns of the majorities in all of Ukraine's eight eastern provinces... It means more than convening peace talks, even if without preconditions... It means getting the United States to invest more effort in drawing all parties toward a political settlement."

That is the heart of the matter: how to convince Washington to give peace a chance – for a change.

Whatever happens, the U.S. taxpayer should refuse to pay a dime for any of this horror.

———

Mr. ROHRABACHER. Mr. Taylor.

STATEMENT OF THE HONORABLE WILLIAM B. TAYLOR, VICE PRESIDENT FOR MIDDLE EAST AND AFRICA, UNITED STATES INSTITUTE OF PEACE (FORMER UNITED STATES AMBASSADOR TO UKRAINE)

Ambassador TAYLOR. Chairman Rohrabacher, Chairman Poe, members of the subcommittees, thank you very much for the opportunity to speak to you today on the shooting down of Malaysia flight 17 and the escalating crisis in Ukraine. I commend you for this timely and important hearing. The views I express today are solely my own. They do not represent those of the United States Institute of Peace because we do not take policy positions.

In my view, today Russia is the single greatest threat to peace in Europe. If the West does not confront this threat, that is, if we appease the Russians now, we will have to confront an even larger threat tomorrow closer to home.

Members of this committee, and my panel members, are very familiar, very aware of the situation in Ukraine. Russian support for the so-called separatists in Donetsk and Luhansk—weapons, leadership, financing, organization, personnel, fighters—is the only thing keeping the Ukrainian Government from establishing security in Southeastern Ukraine. Security is needed to find the remaining victims of the missile strike on the Malaysia airliner and to complete the investigation. Russian support allows the so-called separatists to continue to impede those efforts.

In my view, we must confront the Russian war against Ukraine. This aggression started with the quiet invasion of Crimea last spring. A sham, at-the-end-of-a-rifle referendum was followed by an illegal annexation. The international community should not allow that annexation to stand. Until that situation is resolved to the satisfaction of Ukraine, the Russian Government should pay serious penalties to Ukraine for the temporary loss of income and illegally confiscated assets that would have come to Ukraine from Crimea.

The international community did not confront the Kremlin on Crimea. As a consequence, the Russians continued their aggression in Donetsk and Luhansk. The leaders of the separatist movement unit have become almost exclusively Russian. Russian equipment continues to flow across the border unimpeded. This equipment, including sophisticated anti-aircraft weapons, shot down the Malaysian airliner, killing 298 people. No matter what individual separatist pushed the button to fire the weapon, let's be clear, Mr. Chairman, the tragedy is Russian responsibility.

What should be done? First, human decency requires the return of the victims to their families. Further, experts need access to the crash site to complete the investigation. If the so-called separatists continue to impede these efforts, the international community, led by the Dutch, Australians, and Malaysians, supported by other nations with victims on MH–17, including the United States, and with the approval of the Ukrainians, should provide an armed international security force to protect the investigators and allow them to find victims and complete their investigation. That investigation should lead to criminal prosecutions of those found responsible.

Second, the international community, led by the United States, should provide Ukraine with the means to eliminate the separatist forces in their country. This means weapons, military advice, intelligence, and financial support to pay and equip their soldiers.

Third, the international community should follow the individual travel bans and asset freezes with harsh economic sanctions on entire sectors of the Russian economy to deter the Kremlin from continued support to the separatists, to force them to close their border to weapons, fighters, and military support, and to pressure them to return Crimea to Ukraine.

Fourth, the international community, led by the United States, should provide financial support to Ukraine as it simultaneously confronts Russian aggression and undertakes serious economic and political reform. The International Monetary Fund loans may have to be increased. Bilateral support will have to be expanded. Advice on economic reform, energy pricing, and anti-corruption in particular, will be needed.

Fifth, the international community should respect Ukraine's right to decide with whom to associate politically and economically. Western political and security institutions, specifically the European Union and NATO, should be open to membership applications from Ukraine.

Mr. Chairman, it is a tragedy that it took the shooting down of a civilian airliner over Ukraine to force the international community to confront Russian aggression. If we don't confront it now, it is appeasement, and Russia will not stop at Donetsk.

Thank you, and I am happy to answer your questions.

Mr. ROHRABACHER. Thank you very much for your testimony.

[The prepared statement of Ambassador Taylor follows:]

United States Institute of Peace

. . .

An independent institution established by Congress to strengthen the nation's capacity
to promote peaceful resolution to international conflicts

. . .

"The Shootdown of Malaysian Flight 17 and the Escalating Crisis in Ukraine"

Testimony before a Joint Subcommittee Hearing

Committee on Foreign Affairs

Subcommittee on Europe, Eurasia and Emerging Threats

Subcommittee on Terrorism, Nonproliferation, and Trade

U.S. House of Representatives

William B. Taylor

United States Institute of Peace

July 29, 2014

Chairman Rohrabacher, Chairman Poe, members of the subcommittees, thank you for the opportunity to present my views on the shooting down of Malaysian Flight 17 and the escalating crisis in Ukraine. I commend you for this timely and important hearing.

The views I express today are solely my own and do not represent those of the United States Institute of Peace, which does not take policy positions.

The Situation Today

In my view, Russia is today the single greatest threat to peace in Europe. If the West does not confront this threat—that is, if we appease the Russians now—we will have to confront an even larger threat tomorrow, closer to home.

Members of this committee and your colleagues are fully aware of the situation in Ukraine. Russian support for the separatists in Donetsk and Luhansk-- weapons, leadership, financing, organization, personnel, fighters -- is the only thing keeping the Ukrainian government from establishing security in southeastern Ukraine. Security is needed to find the remaining victims of the missile strike on the Malaysian airliner and to complete the investigation. Russian support allows the separatists to continue to impede those efforts.

In my view we must confront the Russian war against Ukraine. This aggression started with the quiet invasion of Crimea last spring. A sham, at-the-end-of-a-rifle referendum was followed by an illegal annexation. The international community should not allow that annexation to stand. Until that situation is resolved to the satisfaction of Ukraine, the Russian government should pay serious penalties to Ukraine for the temporary loss of income and illegally confiscated assets that would have come to Ukraine from Crimea.

The international community did not confront the Kremlin over Crimea. As a consequence, the Russians continued their aggression in Donetsk and Luhansk. The leaders of the separatist movement have become almost exclusively Russian, and Russian equipment flows across the border unimpeded. This equipment—including sophisticated anti-aircraft weapons—shot down the Malaysian airliner killing 298 people. No matter what individual separatist pushed the button to fire the weapon—let's be clear, Mr. Chairman-- the tragedy is Russian responsibility.

Recommendations

What should be done.

First, human decency requires the return of the victims to their families. Further, experts need access to the crash site to complete the investigation. If the separatists continue to impede these efforts, the international community-- led by the Dutch, Australians and Malaysians; supported by other nations with victims on MH17, including the United States; and with the approval of the Ukrainians—should provide an armed, international security force to protect the investigators and allow them to find the victims and complete their investigation. That investigation should lead to criminal prosecutions of those found responsible.

Second, the international community, led by the United States, should provide Ukraine with the means to eliminate the separatist forces in their country. This means weapons, military advice, intelligence, and financial support to pay and equip their soldiers.

Third, the international community should follow the individual travel bans and asset freezes with harsh economic sanctions on entire sectors of the Russian economy to deter the

Kremlin from continued support to the separatists, to force them to close their border to weapons, fighters and military support, and to pressure them to return Crimea to Ukraine.

Fourth, the international community, led by the United States, should provide financial support to Ukraine as it simultaneously confronts Russian aggression and undertakes serious economic and political reform. The International Monetary Fund loans may have to be increased. Bilateral support will have to be expanded. Advice on economic reform—energy pricing and anti-corruption in particular—will be needed.

Fifth, the international community should respect Ukraine's right to decide with whom to associate politically and economically. Western political and security institutions—specifically, the European Union and NATO—should be open to membership applications from Ukraine.

Mr. Chairman, it is a tragedy that it took the shooting down of a civilian airliner over Ukraine to force the international community to confront Russian aggression. If we don't confront it now, it's appeasement, and Russia will not stop at Donetsk.

Thank you. I am happy to answer your questions.

The views expressed in this testimony are those of the author and not the U.S. Institute of Peace, which does not take policy positions.

Mr. ROHRABACHER. Dr. Aron.

STATEMENT OF LEON ARON, PH.D., RESIDENT SCHOLAR AND DIRECTOR OF RUSSIAN STUDIES, THE AMERICAN ENTERPRISE INSTITUTE

Mr. ARON. Thank you very much, Mr. Chairman. Answering your call to see how the settlement could be reached in Ukraine, I think it is very helpful to look at the sources of Russian behavior and put the conflict in the wider military and political context to see what shapes Mr. Putin's strategy.

From the moment the regime of Viktor Yanukovych was overthrown in Kiev at the end of February, Russia, that is Mr. Vladimir Putin, has pursued three strategic goals in Ukraine. First, to punish, humiliate, destabilize, if possible dismember and ultimately derail a Euro-bound Ukraine. Second, to prevent the West from imposing meaningful, binding sanctions. And finally, to continue to solidify Mr. Putin's domestic political base by rallying around the flag.

This third objective is the most important one. By all indications, Mr. Putin is engineering a Presidency for life. This is not an easy task in a Russia with a stagnant economy, possibly sliding in recession, rising food prices, enormous corruption, and continuing decline in the quality of education, health care, and upward mobility. As recently as the end of 2013, according to public opinion polls, the Russian people's trust in Putin's promises, his popularity, and the desire to see him President again in 2018 were at record lows.

All, however, was forgiven and forgotten in the deafening din of the monopolistic propaganda that followed the annexation of Crimea and the by-proxy invasion of east-south Ukraine. The patriotic euphoria at the sight of these alleged victories, for the alleged just cause of saving the ethic brethren from the depredation of what Moscow continues to call the Nazi junta in Kiev, combined with an equally unbridled paranoia of the NATO plots from which only President Putin is capable of shielding the motherland, all of that has proven irresistible.

But there is something else that interfered with Mr. Vladimir Putin's success, and that is the unexpected Ukrainian advance on the battlefield, which created big political problems for Putin. As I have mentioned, the effort of the Russian domestic propaganda machine has been very successful. But if one lives by propagandistic hysteria, one may also die or at least be bled by it. The propaganda-induced mood cannot be tamped down quickly to justify giving up on the forces of civil self-defense, as the Kremlin continues to call its proxies in Ukraine.

Therefore, a retreat from, not to mention a defeat in Ukraine is not a political option for Mr. Putin. So in the face of the Ukrainian advance, from the beginning of July, Russia in effect has imposed a no-fly zone over east-south Ukraine, and that is the political and military context in which the tragedy of the downing of MH–17 has occurred.

Now, where from now, as far as Russia is concerned? Well, if the efforts to stop the Ukrainian advance with a no-fly zone, as well as the accelerated movement of troops and heavy equipment across the border, which has been mentioned here already, fail, Mr. Putin may declare Ukraine in the throes of a fratricidal civil war and thus necessitating Russia's direct military intervention to protect innocent civilian lives.

In doing so, Mr. Putin is likely to invoke the so-called Libya precedent, which Moscow repeatedly hinted at as a justification for such an action. After all, from their point of view, Moscow would only be following what the West did in Libya in 2011.

This option, however, is not without risks, and the biggest of them is that the Ukrainian Army is likely to put up a fight. And if Russian casualties begin to multiply, Putin's domestic support may begin to erode very quickly, because over half of the Russians, according to public opinion polls, repeatedly told the pollsters that they do not want Russia to invade Ukraine directly.

Therefore, it seems to me that Vladimir Putin's preferred choice is likely to be a call for an immediate cessation of hostilities, and, as it has done repeatedly in the past, Moscow will call also for direct negotiations between Kiev and it proxies.

Now, there is nothing inherently wrong with that, in fact that should be welcomed, except we have reasons to doubt that the real peace rather than victory in Ukraine is the goal, because such a cease-fire will enable Russian separatists to stay in control of the territories they hold today and Russia's proposed truce would allow Russia to have its cake and eat it, too. It will stop the Ukrainian offensive, it will save the proxies from defeat, while at the same time avoiding resorting to the direct invasion by Russian regular troops.

And so whatever the actual tactics, Russia's strategy will continue to be shaped by the fact that a successful low-intensity war in Ukraine is a key domestic political imperative of the Putin regime. That, in turn, makes not the prospect for peace, but a bloody stalemate as the likeliest outcome in the short and perhaps even medium term.

Thank you very much.

[The prepared statement of Mr. Aron follows:]

Leon Aron, Ph.D.

Russia's Next Moves in Ukraine

Submitted for the record as written testimony before the Subcommittee on Europe, Eurasia and Emerging Threats and Subcommittee on Terrorism, Nonproliferation, and Trade of the Foreign Affairs Committee, the U.S. House of Representatives, June 29, 2014

From the moment the corrupt pro-Russian authoritarian regime of Viktor Yanukovich was overthrown in Kiev at the end of February, Russia, that is Vladimir Putin, has pursued three strategic goals: First, to punish, humiliate, destabilize, if possible, dismember and, ultimately, derail a Europe-bound Ukraine. Second, to prevent the West from imposing meaningful, biting sanctions. And finally, to continue to solidify Putin's domestic political base by means of the rally around the flag effect.

The third objective is the most important one. By all indications, Putin is engineering a presidency-for-life. This is a not an easy task in a Russia with a stagnant economy and possible slide into recession, rising food prices, enormous corruption and continuing decline in the quality of education and health care. As recently as the end of 2013, according to public opinion polls, the Russian people's trust in his promises, his popularity, and the desire to see him as president again in 2018 all were at record lows of Putin's effectively 14 years in power.

All however was forgiven and forgotten in the deafening din of the monopolistic propaganda that followed the annexation of Crimea and the by-proxy invasion of east-south Ukraine. The patriotic euphoria at the sight of these victories for the "just cause" of "saving the ethnic brethren" from depredations by the "Nazi junta" in Kiev combined with an equally unbridled paranoia of NATO plots, from which only President Putin is capable of shielding the Motherland have proved irresistible.

Yet newly elected Ukrainian President Petro Poroshenko has quickly proved surprisingly successful not only in mobilizing political support for confronting the Russian proxies, but also in rebuilding the completely demoralized and beggared Ukrainian armed forces. By early July he managed to engineer what looks like a successful Ukrainian ground offensive to recover sovereignty over the country's industrial heartland, starting with the rebel stronghold of Slavyansk on July 7.

The unexpected Ukrainian advance has created a big political problem for Putin. As I have mentioned, the effort of the Russian domestic monopolistic propaganda machine has been very effective. But if one lives by propagandistic hysteria, one may also die, or at least be bled by it. The propaganda-induced mood cannot be tamped down quickly to justify giving up on the "forces of civil self-defense," as the Kremlin calls an assorted rabble, armed and supplied by Moscow, and led and trained by professional Russian special troops, intelligence officers as well as Chechen and Cossack mercenaries. Putin knows only too well the history of the former Serbian strongman, Slobodan Milosevic, who had ridden similarly high in his fight against what he called Bosnia "jihadists" and Croatian "Catholic Nazi Ustashas" until he retreated.

Thus, retreat from, not to mention defeat in, Ukraine is not an option for Putin. So in the face of the Ukrainian advance since the beginning of July, Russia, in effect, has imposed a no-fly zone over east-south Ukraine.

This is the political and military context in which followed the downing of a Ukrainian military cargo plane and fighter jet earlier in the same week that Malaysian Airlines Flight MH17 was shot down by a Buk M-1 (the SA-11 Gadfly in the NATO designation) surface-to-air-missile, fired from the Ukrainian side of the border. Last Wednesday, two Ukrainian SU-25 fighter jets were downed as well. Simultaneously, Russia has escalated the movement of men and heavy equipment across its border with Ukraine, including Grad multiple launch rocket systems, T-64 tanks, infantry combat vehicles with automatic cannons and armored personnel carriers. At the same time Russian artillery began to pound Ukrainian army positions.

If these efforts notwithstanding Russia fails to stop the Ukrainian advance, Putin will be facing two options. First, he may declare that Ukraine "in the throes of a fratricidal civil war" necessitates Russia's direct military intervention to protect "innocent civilian lives." In doing so, Putin is likely to invoke the "Libya precedent," which Moscow repeatedly hinted at as a justification for such an action: after all, Russia will only be following what the West did in Libya in 2011.

This option, however, is not without risks. First, the Ukrainian army is likely to put up a fight and, if Russian casualties begin to multiply, Putin's domestic support may begin to erode quickly seeing that the almost half of Russians have repeatedly told pollsters that they do not want Russia to invade Ukraine.

Thus Putin's preferred choice is likely to be a call for an immediate "cessation of hostilities" and, as it has done repeatedly in the past, "direct negotiations" between Kiev and its proxies. The West is also likely to put strong pressure on Ukraine to comply in the hopes of preventing the first open invasion of a major European country since the end of World War II 69 years ago

Needless to say, by enabling the pro-Russian "separatists" to stay in control of the territories they hold today, the Russia-proposed "truce" would allow Russia to have its cake and eat it too: stopping the Ukrainian offensive and saving its proxies from defeat without resorting to an open invasion by regular troops.

The longer the truce, not to mention negotiations, the weaker the support for the activist Ukrainian president Petro Poroshenko will be and the lesser the chance for an economic recovery in Ukraine. Given Ukraine's post-Soviet political history, such a "frozen conflict" could lead to yet another cycle of domestic political instability and perhaps eventually to the realization of the Russian strategic goal of de-railing a Europe-bound Ukrainian regime. In the meantime, the truce can be quickly broken by the "rebels" on orders from Moscow, just as the most recent unilateral Ukrainian ceasefire was at the beginning of July.

Whatever the actual tactics, Russia's strategy will continue to be shaped by the fact that a successful low-intensity war on Ukraine is a key domestic political imperative of the Putin regime.

This, in turn, makes a protracted and bloody stalemate the likeliest outcome in both the short and perhaps medium term of the Ukrainian crisis.

Mr. ROHRABACHER. Well, I want to thank all of our witnesses. We have as not as broad a range of opinion as I would have liked to have had, although we have differences of opinion in the panel.

I plan to ask my 5 minutes worth of questions and then we will give my other colleagues a chance.

First of all, do we agree that this was not an intentional shootdown of this airline? Does everyone agree to that? I mean, nobody said, let's shoot down a commercial airline.

With that said, there are—not counting the victims of this airline—did we say there were 800 people who have been killed since February?

Mr. SALVIA. According to the New York Times of yesterday, they gave a figure of 800 since April.

Mr. ROHRABACHER. Okay. Is that figure about right with the rest of you?

Ambassador TAYLOR. It is probably more like 1,000.

Mr. ROHRABACHER. Probably more.

Of those who are dead, how many are civilians from the eastern part of Ukraine who have been killed by the military operations by the Ukrainian Government in that region, of the dead? Of that 800 dead, are we talking about half of them? Or the vast majority of them?

Mr. ARON. Mr. Chairman, it is very difficult in the conditions of the urban warfare, it is very difficult to establish which side killed how many people. And the propaganda efforts on both sides are tremendous.

Mr. ROHRABACHER. So would you agree with that, Mr. Salvia, that it is hard to tell?

Mr. SALVIA. Absolutely, yes.

Mr. ROHRABACHER. It seems to me that it wouldn't be that hard to tell. It seems to me that if you have dead civilians on the ground in Eastern Ukraine that you would have to assume that they were not being shot by, intentionally, by the separatists who are there as part of their community. That would seem to be that way.

Ambassador TAYLOR. Mr. Chairman, it is hard to tell. We don't know. But what we do know is that we have recently seen that the separatists have killed civilians and put them in a grave, in a mass grave. We found this over the last couple of days.

Mr. ROHRABACHER. The separatists killed the civilians?

Ambassador TAYLOR. Yes, sir.

Mr. ROHRABACHER. For what reason did they do that?

Ambassador TAYLOR. We don't know, sir. What we know is there are some dead people.

Mr. ROHRABACHER. Have there been any cease-fires in this between the separatists and the Ukrainian Army? There have been?

Mr. ARON. There have been cease-fires.

Mr. ROHRABACHER. How many cease-fires have there been?

Mr. ARON. There were several. But the latest one, if you remember, Mr. Chairman, the latest one is of course because of MH–17. It was a unilateral cease-fire. But the one before ended when the separatists attacked the Donetsk airport. It was a unilateral cease-fire by Ukraine, and it was broken by the separatists.

Mr. ROHRABACHER. Okay. So there have been cease-fires. Do you agree with that, Mr. Salvia?

Mr. SALVIA. Your question? I am sorry? Will you repeat the question?

Mr. ROHRABACHER. How many cease-fires do we know of there?

Mr. SALVIA. Well, the main one was the one Dr. Aron was referring to, which was June 20th to June 30th. So it was a tentative cease-fire, but that then ended in renewed fighting.

Mr. ROHRABACHER. Okay. Have there been other cease-fires?

Mr. SALVIA. Brief ones. Again, as Dr. Aron said. After the immediate shootdown of the airplane there was a brief one. There has not been a prolonged cease-fire coupled with serious negotiations.

Mr. ROHRABACHER. I think your point that we have been calling for cease-fires in Palestine, Israeli cease-fires, we don't seem to be putting that type of energy into calling for cease-fires and negotiations in Ukraine.

Is this issue one of where people are demanding federalism and there is not a negotiation on this issue? Or is this just a matter of the people are just demanding that they have a separate status, totally separate status, and become independent of Ukraine? The people who are actually fighting, what demand have they made?

Mr. BRZEZINSKI. Sir, I guess my impression is, is that while there is generally always a demand for more autonomy from regions——

Mr. ROHRABACHER. Yes.

Mr. BRZEZINSKI [continuing]. This conflict wasn't created by Ukrainians seeking greater autonomy. It was created by Russian operatives who were sent into Eastern Ukraine and seized buildings and violently closed off the region.

Mr. ROHRABACHER. So the people who are seizing buildings, the first buildings that were seized that I remember in Ukraine were seized by the people who were trying to force the democratically elected President out of his office, seizing buildings in the western part of Ukraine. And I am sure those were local people, although there has been the suggestions that they were very radical. And so buildings were seized there.

Do you agree, Doctor, with that analysis, that the people who were basically starting this and seizing those buildings originally were all Russian agents and not local people?

Mr. SALVIA. Well, I don't know. I think that may go a bit far. I mean, it certainly is true what you say that a lot of this originated last winter when you had the efforts to overthrow what you correctly say was the democratically elected Government of Ukraine, a government which faced elections in February 2015.

In other words, if the opposition in Ukraine was upset with what Yanukovych did about the European Association Agreement, they had a whole year to organize, to deal with the matter at the ballot box. After all, the Maidan movement, which I was hugely sympathetic to myself, personally, was all about European values. Well, what are European, Western values but democratic elections? Elections were coming.

Unfortunately, it didn't go that way. And those elections could have been monitored by Western monitors to see if there was any kind of vote fraud, had they occurred. We saw what happened in 2004 during the Orange Revolution when there was vote fraud and our Western monitors found it and they brought it to light. That could have happened again. You could have had a democratic process taking place and these issues dealt with that way.

Instead, to get to your point, a violent solution was opted for. And I was in the Maidan in February, saw young guys running around town with spears and pikes and sharpened metallic objects. There were huge military tents in Maidan with crate after crate of Molotov cocktail mix. What were these guys doing with that stuff? Where did they get it?

In any case, so you had the violent overthrow of the government. And then the uprisings in the west, Lviv declared itself a Party-of-Regions-free-zone and that kind of thing. This was all seen as hugely provocative in the East.

Mr. ROHRABACHER. The most important thing that you are bringing out is that the violence that we are talking about did not start with the separatists taking over a building in the eastern part of Ukraine, although that was a violent act. And the military coming in to then make sure that those buildings were not occupied, but instead were under the sovereignty of the Kiev government created more violence.

There is one other question I had that was specifically—oh, yeah. The question that was posed, and I believe by one of the other panelists, was that if indeed Yanukovych would have signed this agreement with Russia rather than the European agreement which was offered, which he didn't feel was as good an agreement, could the Ukrainian people in the next election cycle, which would have been 2 years away, eliminated that agreement and eliminated—well, they could have eliminated Yanukovych, obviously—through the ballot box or was this agreement a situation that there was no democratic alternative to counteract because it would have been permanent?

Mr. SALVIA. Let me just say that what Yanukovych did was he said no to the Russian Eurasian Customs Union. He said no to that, right? He said yes to the European Association Agreement, though pending revision, because he said this is radically not in our interest, I am not going to sign in Vilnius, we won't sign that. And he also said that the European incentive package was completely inadequate, of $800 million, contingent on renewed IMF funding, which he didn't want to do.

Mr. ROHRABACHER. Well, whatever agreement that he signed with Russia, could the people of Ukraine have elected a Parliament that would have eliminated that 2 years down the road?

Mr. SALVIA. I think so, because the agreement that Putin was offering him at that time was—again, Yanukovych rejected the Russian deal of entering the Eurasian Customs Union. So there was no treaty or anything like that. What Putin was offering was a financing deal, saying $20 billion coming to you and a cut in gas prices. That was a simple deal, and that could have been reversed or not.

Mr. ROHRABACHER. First of all, we hope that the violence that now plagues Ukraine, that there is not only a cease-fire, but that there is a cessation, that people with this airline catastrophe where you had so many innocent people lost their lives just from a commercial airliner, let's hope that this jars people to the point that they sit down and take nonviolent options seriously and negotiation seriously with each other. That is not the case, if Mr. Brzezinski is correct, that this is basically an outside-motivated violent episode, and it is not just erupting from the inside.

I happen to think that this started when Yanukovych was overthrown with violence, and that is the point it started. Whether or not that means that now outsiders have taken over the situation and that Ukrainians themselves are not going to be able to do this, come to an understanding, I hope that we play a positive role in bringing that together. And I would hope that if Russia is indeed fanning the flames rather than trying to just react to other violence that is going on, I would hope that the Russian Government sees a way to start bringing peace to Ukraine as well. I hope that we would submit that to them and their conscience and turn a spotlight on it in the world.

So I now yield to my ranking member, Mr. Keating.

Mr. KEATING. Thank you, Mr. Chairman.

Mr. Salvia, I noticed in your comments the absence of Russian involvement conspicuously in this. And you are pointing the finger at the constitutional government's repression of the national population and Washington's obsession with Russia.

Now, I want to learn a little bit more about your organization, the American Institute in Ukraine. I want to ask you a question, how it was founded, who is funding it, where it is headquartered—I couldn't find a site—where it is based. Just briefly. What is the American Institute in Ukraine?

Mr. SALVIA. It is a nonprofit organization. It is a very small group. It is myself and a partner working with a media group in Kiev that put on roundtable discussions in Kiev, at least until recently. It has been kind of hard to operate——

Mr. KEATING. So it is headquartered in Kiev?

Mr. SALVIA. Well, you know——

Mr. KEATING. Is it registered as a foreign agent?

Mr. SALVIA. We had an office in Kiev.

Mr. KEATING. Are you registered as a foreign agent, then?

Mr. SALVIA. In Kiev? Where?

Mr. KEATING. Here. If you were in Kiev, are you registered as a foreign agent? Yes or no?

Mr. SALVIA. We don't represent——

Mr. KEATING. Yes or no?

Mr. SALVIA. No.

Mr. KEATING. Do you have a 501(c)(3), since you are a nonprofit? We couldn't find any.

Mr. SALVIA. I believe it is a 501(c)(6).

Mr. KEATING. You have that as a nonprofit?

Mr. SALVIA. Yes.

Mr. KEATING. Okay. Now, I want to talk to you about the institute, too, because you mentioned you have other partners. You have two principals, Mr. Jatras and Mr. Spinck, that are also with the Global Strategic Communications Group, and they are in management positions with that.

Now, this organization, along with the two principals I mentioned, currently were registered lobbyists and/or registered foreign agents. You have had those for clients, that group. Is that correct? Yes or no?

Mr. SALVIA. Agents for what group?

Mr. KEATING. Global Strategic Communications Group, which you and your principals you just mentioned. I want to find out about that group.

Mr. SALVIA. But you mentioned something specifically about one of them was working for whom?

Mr. KEATING. I want to know if that organization I just mentioned, along with the two principals I mentioned, are currently or were in the past registered lobbyists for foreign agents and for other clients, including a former Prime Minister of Ukraine, including the deputy, Russian Federation State Duma and his party, and including Russian corporations.

Let me be more specific so I just get a yes or no from you. In 2005, the Foreign Agents Registration Act had some information, and it said that organization served as the PR arm for Deputy Prime Minister of the Russian Federation Dmitry Rogozin and his Rodina party. Further, there is another FARA inclusion that declares that it is associating with members of your organization with the now ousted President Yanukovych of Ukraine. Is that correct, yes or no?

Mr. SALVIA. Yes. One of the——

Mr. KEATING. That is correct, yes.

Mr. SALVIA. One of the members of the group was giving advice to Yanukovych.

Mr. KEATING. I just want the public to know. I am asking the questions. I just wanted the public to know for transparency reasons why your remarks, which were so conspicuously absent Russian involvement, may have been absent that.

And I just want to go further, if I could, and just say this. I want one more question as well.

The Kaalbye Shipping International, Kaalbye Shipping International has been listed as a client of Global Strategic Communication Group as well. Now, is that the same Kaalbye Shipping International which was implicated in the illegal transfer of Russian arms to Syria, Iran, Sudan, and other countries of concern? Is that the same? Yes or no?

Mr. SALVIA. Sir, I am not familiar with that whole thing. I am just not familiar with it. Sorry, sir.

Mr. KEATING. Well, perhaps I can enlighten.

I have some documents I would like placed in the record, Mr. Chairman. If I have unanimous consent to place those reinforcing documents in the record.

Mr. ROHRABACHER. May I ask a clarification to your question? Are you questioning him about the American Institute in Ukraine or about another——

Mr. KEATING. I am questioning, Mr. Chairman, about both. Because this hearing should be transparent, unlike——

Mr. ROHRABACHER. Okay. Excuse me. Excuse me. What was the other organization you are asking about?

Mr. KEATING. The other organization was the organization that our witness said the principals were indeed involved with that he mentioned, the same as the American Institution Group, and that is the Global Strategic Communications Group.

Mr. ROHRABACHER. Is he affiliated with that group?

Mr. KEATING. Yes, he is. Let him answer.

Yes or no, sir?

Mr. SALVIA. Well, I think the question was, did one of——

Mr. KEATING. This is my time, by the way, Mr. Chairman.

Mr. ROHRABACHER. Sure.

Mr. KEATING. Can I reclaim the time——

Mr. ROHRABACHER. Yes, you may.

Mr. KEATING [continuing]. That you interrupted me?

Mr. ROHRABACHER. Yeah. Right.

Mr. SALVIA. The question was, did one of the members of the group have anything to do the former Prime Minister of the Ukraine——

Mr. ROHRABACHER. No. Are you involved with that specific organization that he is asking about?

Mr. KEATING. Mr. Chairman, with all due respect, it is my time to question. And I did question him, and he did indicate that.

So I just want the public to know, I want the world to know that the comments you gave that conspicuously left out Russia for any involvement and pointed the finger at Washington and at the constitutionally elected Government of Ukraine, I want them to know who you and who this organization is.

That is all I have to say. He answered my question, so I yield back, Mr. Chairman.

Oh, Mr. Chairman, one other point of order.

Mr. ROHRABACHER. Go right ahead.

Mr. KEATING. Pending is my request, unanimous consent, to make this reinforcing information part of the committee hearing's record.

Mr. ROHRABACHER. Hearing no objection, whatever you would like to put in the record.

Mr. KEATING. Thank you, Mr. Chairman.

Mr. ROHRABACHER. Are you a member of that organization? Are you an employee or an actual member of the organization he was referring to?

Mr. SALVIA. Not an employee. Not an employee of the organization. But some of the guys in the group have——

Mr. ROHRABACHER. No, no, I am talking about you, are you a member of that organization?

Mr. SALVIA. No.

Mr. KEATING. Mr. Chairman, point of order. You interrupted me. I have a document that I submitted where he is listed as the director for the Global Strategic Communications Group.

Mr. ROHRABACHER. Okay.

Mr. SALVIA. Oh, I thought you were talking about this Kaalbye— I am sorry, I thought you were talking about this Kaalbye business or something.

Mr. ROHRABACHER. The question is, are you a director of that organization.

Mr. SALVIA. Global Strategic Communications Group does consulting, public advocacy consulting on behalf of clients, whatever they may be.

Mr. ROHRABACHER. Okay. So are you a director?

Mr. SALVIA. Yeah, I have to do with it, yes.

Mr. ROHRABACHER. Okay. Thank you. That is important.

Let me just again note, however, that my ranking member, while doing a very good job as, which is his profession, as a prosecutor, let me just note that we didn't actually talk about any specific areas of disagreement. And, quite frankly, I am disappointed that instead of talking about ideas and information to find out accuracy, that instead we sought to attack the witness.

Mr. KEATING. Mr. Chairman, if I may.

Mr. ROHRABACHER. You may answer that.

Mr. KEATING. Because it is point of personal privilege.

Thank you for your continued cooperation in our relationship. And I am not disappointed in our relationship. But I must tell you, if we have a witness who is testifying that information and informing the public, we should know who that witness is.

I yield back.

Mr. ROHRABACHER. Yes. And you spent your time what we call poisoning the well.

Mr. KEATING. Mr. Chairman, I take point of personal privilege with that.

Mr. ROHRABACHER. Okay. Go right ahead.

Mr. KEATING. What I did was, I think, uncover the cloud and the shroud that this witness had in terms of a prejudice, and the public should know that if we are to conduct the kind of transparent hearing that this Congress and this country is noted for.

Mr. ROHRABACHER. Yes, I think all things should be transparent, and I think when we have hearings that we should be focusing on ideas and information that can help us determine what the reality is and find different avenues to find solutions to the problems we face. And I think that no matter what witness we have, we can find our time spending our time trying to basically attack the witness or attack the ideas the witness is expressing. And I am not saying that attacking the witness' credibility is not a viable methodology of dealing with political challenges like this. That is not the way I handle myself. But I think that it is better to confront ideas than it is to confront personalities.

Your honor, would you like to——

Mr. POE. I suspect the chairman of the full committee ought to be next. I will wait my turn.

Mr. ROHRABACHER. So ordered.

Mr. Royce.

Mr. ROYCE. Thank you, Mr. Chairman.

Thank you, Judge Poe.

One of the advantages of having a vibrant press is that you get to watch on television things unfold not always as they were planned. And we saw in Kharkiv, we saw in that town a group of separatists who stormed the opera house, mistaking it for city hall. Now, one of two possibilities here. One is that people in the town are ambivalent about opera and civics and know neither where the opera house is or city hall is. But I think more likely, since the Russian camera crew was there filming this and filmed the Russian tricolor being put up on the opera house, and then one of the locals said, that is not city hall, and then you got to see them take it back down, run back across town, and you saw the so-called separatists in their masks and such go up and actually put it on city hall and, again, second take, for the Russian camera crew.

The reality here seems to be that you do have a lot of foreign influence coming into the country, as reported to me and Judge Poe when we were in Dnepropetrovsk, that is in the business of putting up Russian flags and in the business of bringing in a great deal of heavy weaponry, as General Breedlove has shared with Congress.

So the question I have, at the end of the day, and I would like each of the panelists to just give me their take, what do you believe President Putin's goals are in Ukraine in all of this? Because this takes a considerable expenditure of resources from Russia in order to finance this kind of an operation.

Ambassador TAYLOR. Mr. Chairman, I would say, I would be interested in the fellow panelists, I would say Mr. Putin would like to have instability in Ukraine so that it cannot pursue the movement toward Europe, movement toward European institutions, that its President, elected overwhelmingly, its people in polls indicate that they would like to do. He would like to cause that instability and is fomenting that instability in Eastern Ukraine.

Mr. ROYCE. I would like to hear the take on every member on the panel.

Mr. ARON. If I may, could I read again from my testimony?

Mr. ROYCE. Sure, Dr. Aron, go ahead.

Mr. ARON. From the moment the regime of Viktor Yanukovich was overthrown in Kiev in the end of February, Russia, that is Vladimir Putin, has pursued three strategic goals. First, to punish, humiliate, destabilize, if possible, dismember, and ultimately derail a Europe-bound Ukraine. Second, to prevent the West from imposing meaningful, biting sanctions. And third, to continue to solidify Mr. Putin's domestic political base by rallying it around the flag.

And I also noted that from my point of view, of somebody who studies Russian politics, I think the third goal is the most important one, because Putin's popularity, trust in him, and most importantly the desire to see him as reelected as President in 2018, by all objective public opinion polls were at record lows at the end of 2013. Now all of those indicators are at record high. That of course is not Russia's privileges. Countries at war rally around the leader. And I think these three goals will continue to motivate Putin.

And which is why, answering Mr. Chairman's call to reach the settlement with Russia, I think we should be realistic about what the goals are. And I think that settlement could be reached, but that would require Vladimir Putin to change the strategy. The problem with changing the strategy is that it is so now intimately and centrally tied to the legitimacy and popularity of his regime that it would be extremely hard for him to change the course.

Mr. ROYCE. And for the remaining two speakers, I mean, watching Russian television and watching this projection of this image, they are beating you, they are beating ethnic Russian speakers, right, that is the theme. But it is not just the theme in Ukraine, it is the theme in the former Soviet states. You see this broadcast into other states, in Central Asia and in the Baltics and in Eastern Europe. So that is the other part of my question. It is not just that this message is directed in Ukraine, it is directed to Russian speakers who are listening across the——

Mr. ARON. I think you are absolutely right. I had a colleague returning recently from Kazakhstan.

Mr. ROYCE. Yes.

Mr. ARON. And as you know, northern Kazakhstan——

Mr. ROYCE. Right.

Mr. ARON [continuing]. Is essentially ethnic Russian. And like Ukraine, Kazakhstan did not exist until the beginning of the Soviet Union. So Putin could say, as he said in his fiery speech following the annexation of Crimea on March 18th of this year to the joint session of the Federal Assembly, which is the Russian Parliament, he could say, well, there was no Kazakhstan. Those were all Russian lands. He said that about Ukraine.

Mr. ROYCE. No. I followed that. But I also followed this story out of Russia that the Ukrainians had supposedly crucified a 3-year-old boy and drug his mother behind a tank. This kind of rhetoric is designed to fire up ethnic Russians to a point where they are thinking emotionally rather than logically.

And it strikes me that because this is going on, not just in Ukraine but elsewhere, it is very important we engage with broadcasting some kind of surrogate—like we did with Radio Free Europe/Radio Liberty in the day when we did it well, we need something that just broadcasts in perspective, a wider perspective on this. They are fueling a rage here which already has led to the downing of one jetliner by having inexperienced separatists who want to wage war, who shot down, I guess, probably 14 planes by now. But that kind of anger that is being generated is going to be a real problem for the region.

Mr. SALVIA. On the question of what Putin would be seeking in Ukraine, I think certainly he wants an agreement on autonomy. In other words, let's put it this way, I think the last thing he wants to do is introduce Russian forces into the country. I think that would be a disaster for him. I think it would be a costly, costly, costly, costly mistake, just in terms of financing it. But politically it would be even more horrendous in terms of poisoning his relationship with Europe, I think in terms of poisoning his relations with Kiev, because ultimately Russia has to have some kind of relationship with Kiev, once all this blows over, when they get back to some kind of normalcy.

So I don't think he wants to do that. I think what he would like to have is some kind of a negotiated thing—I think he has indicated this—an agreement on autonomy, widespread autonomy for the various regions of Ukraine, and things that would take Ukraine out of the equation as some kind of a problem for Russia. In other words, making non-NATO membership part of the Constitution—neutrality or non-aligned status—things like agreement on language rights, so that language rights are protected.

Mr. ROYCE. But all of that would be done by Poroshenko anyway. Poroshenko is in support of language rights, it is very clear.

Mr. SALVIA. Yes.

Mr. ROYCE. And certainly on the NATO issue as well.

But, anyway, my time has expired. And thank you.

Mr. ROHRABACHER. And thank you for joining us, Mr. Chairman.

Whereas there aren't any, with permission, we could go straight to Judge Poe.

Mr. POE. Thank the chairman.

Thank you, gentlemen, for being here.

I want to side my remarks first with the comments from Mr. Keating. It is always good to know the background of witnesses when you are asking witnesses questions to see if there is any motive.

With that said, I would like to address the issues that I talked about in my opening statement, the broader issue, not just the airplane that was shot down, criminally, yes. Hold those people accountable. But going back to what Dr. Aron has said about the motives, the intent, rather, the intent of Putin and the Russians, long-term intent. A statement was made that Russians don't want to put troops in Ukraine because it is expensive. They sure didn't have any trouble putting troops in Georgia, and they are still there.

Mr. Brzezinski, what do you see as the longer-term goal of Putin? I, too, believe that it is nationalistic. The Russians like this invasion of Ukraine. What is it, 40, 50 percent of them support the invasion or support the Russian movement? Putin backs off a little, maybe negotiates with the West, does that not look like weakness to the Russian people? I don't know. I am asking your opinion on long-term goal.

I talked to Moldavian members of Parliament. They think they are next. Maybe not today, maybe not tomorrow, but some day. They think they are next. And of course Poland has always got the problem with the Russians.

Are these fears of Latvia and some of these other countries that they have expressed to Members of Congress, it is not real fears, or is there some substance to Putin's long-term goal, which I think is to make the Russian empire bigger? Would you weigh in on that, please?

Mr. BRZEZINSKI. Yes, sir, Chairman Poe.

First, I would point out that the Russians are not just in Georgia, they are in Ukraine. There are 20,000 to 30,000 Russian troops occupying Crimea. Russian special forces are leading and fighting in Eastern Ukraine. Russian political operatives are the head of the separatist republics in Russia. So Russia is in Ukraine militarily and illegitimately in political ways.

What is President Putin's goal? President Putin's goal is essentially a revanchist vision. He wants to reestablish Russian greatness. And he finds that greatness——

Mr. POE. Sort of like the czar.

Mr. BRZEZINSKI. Sort of like the czar. Like Czar Peter.

Mr. POE. Czar Vladimir, Czar Vladimir Putin.

Mr. BRZEZINSKI. His vision is to recreate Russian influence over the sphere of the former Soviet Union, including the Warsaw Pact, for that matter. And what is particularly dangerous about that vision is he is reintroducing into Europe the principle of ethnic sovereignty. That he, that Russia, has a unilateral right to go in and redraw borders simply because there are ethnic Russians living across those borders. That is incredibly dangerous, that principle.

Mr. POE. That is his so-called legal justification for invading his neighbors. Would you say that is right?

Mr. BRZEZINSKI. That is correct.

Mr. POE. He is not really going to promote humanitarian goals in Eastern Ukraine, he is going over there to take back Ukraine and make it part of Russia. I mean, is that oversimplification?

Mr. BRZEZINSKI. I think that is pretty accurate. I would put his priorities first in terms specifically with Ukraine is to subordinate Ukraine.

Mr. POE. Long term, I have just a few minutes left, long term what do you see?

Mr. BRZEZINSKI. Subordinate Ukraine under Russian influence. If he can't do that, keep Ukraine unstable, destabilized, so it can't go to the West and in a minimum carve up parts of Ukraine that are strategically important to him, including Eastern Ukraine and Southern Ukraine.

Mr. POE. Mr. Taylor, weigh in on the same question. Long term, what do you see Putin's goals are?

Ambassador TAYLOR. Mr. Chairman, I don't think he is that strategic of a thinker. I think he is an opportunist. He saw an opportunity to go into Crimea and he did. He could do it and he did. He did it easily, quietly, illegally, totally illegally. I don't think it is a legal rationale that he is trying to establish about protecting Russians. That is not legal. Indeed, that led to World War I when the Serbians tried to indicate——

Mr. POE. I am not saying he is right. He is trying to justify it to the world.

Ambassador TAYLOR. He is trying to justify it, but it is not a legal justification. He may be trying make that case.

So in answer to your question, Mr. Chairman, I don't know what his long-term goals are. I am not sure he does. I think he is taking advantage of weakness. He is taking advantage of the fact that, so far, the West has not confronted him, and he is going to move until we confront him.

Mr. POE. Dr. Aron, long-term goals. I appreciate your three bullet points, but what do you see down the road?

Mr. ARON. Well, even a longer-term, wider context. A year ago I published an article in Foreign Affairs called "The Putin Doctrine." And I think it is very simple. It is to recover geostrategic, economic, political, and cultural assets lost in the fall of the Soviet Union.

In other words, he does not want to recreate the Soviet Union. It is silly, it is costly, it is risky. But he wants to recreate or take control of the assets inside the country. He already did. Over politics. Over the key aspects of the economy, oil and gas. Over culture.

And in the broader sense, I think, in the territory of the former Soviet Union, is to establish Russia as being in control, not just hegemonic power, but in control of the former Soviet states. That does not involve occupation of every former Soviet state. It involves, as Ian pointed out, it involves keeping those states' foreign policies, and sometimes even domestic policies, bound to approval or disapproval from Moscow.

Mr. POE. Let me interrupt there, since I am out of time.

Mr. ARON. I am done. Thank you.

Mr. POE. So he would use a bigger approach than just militarily. He could use economic approach, like he is using in Eastern Europe and part of Western Europe with the monopoly of Gazprom, for example, because there is no competition. He can shut off the gas in Ukraine, which he has done, and I was there when he did it in the winter, and it was cold and it was dark.

So that opportunity, United States, Western powers who think that this aggression should be stopped, maybe we should have some responses economically, as well as helping out Ukrainians militarily with helping them solve their own security crisis. Would you agree with that or not?

Mr. ARON. In connection with economic measures, and also apparently there are going to be some serious sanctions rolled out, a word of caution. Precisely because, as I said in my testimony, war in Ukraine is a domestic Russian political issue. It has become one. It is at the center of this regime. It is responsible for a great deal of legitimacy and popularity. Don't expect sanctions to work quickly.

In fact, in the short term, I think they are going to cause Putin doubling down, if I know the man correctly, doubling down in Ukraine, rallying around the flag, his popularity even going higher. Long term, medium term, probably, probably they will force him to make choices. But don't oversell economic sanctions for now.

Mr. POE. I yield back.

Mr. ROHRABACHER. Thank you very much, Your Honor.

Next we have Representative Duncan.

Mr. DUNCAN. Thank you, Mr. Chairman. Thanks for having this important hearing.

As I sat here and listened to the testimony and the questioning, I have to ask, what is the correct level of outrage from the free world to this tragedy? And have we seen it? We see global protest over Israel defending its right to exist and its self-defense, but we don't see global outrage over the use of a weapon of war to shoot down a commercial airliner.

And think about this: 300, plus or minus, passengers lost their lives, basically one-third of the total lives lost in Gaza, where is the world outrage? This is rhetorical, but what is the appropriate response from the free world? And what is, we will just say, the historic leader of the free world, what is the appropriate response to this egregious act of aggression which cost the lives, truly innocent lives on a commercial airliner?

This act was committed with a very sophisticated weapon. If they could hold this sign back up real quick. This was an SA–11 missile, a weapon of war, and a sophisticated launcher. This isn't Charlie Wilson's war with Afghanis running up with shoulder-fired stingers, fire-and-forget missiles. This has sophisticated radar. It takes sophisticated training in order to operate it. This wasn't some rebel that just happened to seize a weapon on the battlefield and use to it shoot down an airliner. I believe it took a little bit more than that. I believe Russia was involved in some way. This isn't a fire-and-forget weapon.

And so I have to ask Mr. Brzezinski, is it likely that Russia would ever let such powerful weapons as this SA–11 out of its full control?

Mr. BRZEZINSKI. I think it is pretty clear it did. I mean, all reports indicate that Russia did transfer SA–11s to the separatists. I think it is an incredibly irresponsible act. Not only did a system like that put innocent airliners at risk, but it probably put Russians forces at risk. So I am stunned, but it is clear he did it.

Mr. DUNCAN. I am, too. I really am stunned that they didn't verify the target before they pulled the trigger. But that is sort of a debatable issue.

Doesn't that support the notion that Russia must have been aware what it was being used for?

Mr. BRZEZINSKI. It is not clear exactly what the command-and-control arrangements were over those systems. But what is clear is that the transfer of the SA–11s was part and parcel of a broader effort by the Russians to intensify their support to the separatists. After each set of sanctions there has been an incremental increase in kind of material support and personnel support Russia has provided the separatists. It really intensified in the last couple of weeks where we have seen columns of APCs, mortars, and tanks cross the Russian-Ukrainian border into the separatists.

And I think the Russians are being driven to do this in part because they see the separatists failing. So what they are trying do right now is desperately consolidate the territory the separatists have so they can lock this into a frozen conflict. And that would, one, perpetuate their ability to keep Ukraine destabilized. And if Ukraine is unstable, it is not going to be able to push its way forward into Europe.

Mr. DUNCAN. So let me ask you this. What is the correct response? How should the Western world, the free world respond to this egregious act?

Mr. BRZEZINSKI. We have to act, we have to respond with resolve and determination. A long time ago, we should have been imposing sectoral sanctions on Russia, body slamming the Russian economy, hitting its financial and energy sectors in particular. That hasn't been done. We have had incremental sanctions, we have had hesitancy. Our military actions have been symbolic at best—a company in Poland, a company in the Baltics, a few planes here.

The Russians mobilized over 100,000 people on the western military district, the western frontier, so to speak, when they began their invasion of Ukraine. That is how serious they were. The West hasn't responded that way, and the result has been Putin has been continuously emboldened in his effort to subordinate and carve up Ukraine.

Mr. DUNCAN. I visited Europe. I met with the Europeans last year. They have been concerned for well over a year at their reliance on Russian gas. Ukraine is definitely concerned about its reliance on gas.

Can't this administration and this government and the Western world with the expedition of LNG terminals and the export of natural gas, which we have an abundance of, not send the right economic signal that Europe is going to lessen its dependence on a foreign source of energy, Ukraine is going to end its dependence on a foreign source of energy, other than the United States? Wouldn't that send the right signal?

Mr. BRZEZINSKI. Yes, sir. Two points. One, LNG would be an important long-term effort to help Ukraine and for that matter Central Europe wean itself from its dependency upon Russian gas exports. In the near term it would be a strong political signal and it would create momentum that would kind of facilitate investment to build the necessary infrastructure for that.

The second point I would make is what amazes me about the West's response economically to this invasion in the Ukraine is the weakness of that response in light of the power balance between the West and Russia. The EU is a $12-trillion economy. It has got a $12-trillion annual GDP. It is globally integrated. It gets approximately 30 percent of its imported gas, not total use of gas, but imported gas from Russia.

Russia is a $2-trillion gas station. It has only got one customer, the EU. It is dependent upon primarily the EU for foreign investment. The EU is also backed by a $16-trillion U.S. economy. So it is amazing how a $2-trillion gas station that is on weak legs can bully around the West, which has well over 6 times its economic magnitude.

I can only explain that by strategic shortsightedness, moral fecklessness, to allow a major European country to be walked over, invaded by Russia, and corporate greed.

Mr. DUNCAN. Well, thank you for that.

Chairman Poe, I am sorry that you were cold in Ukraine, but we cold take care of that by exporting gas from the United States to friends and allies around the world who want U.S. gas and lessen their dependence on Russia. And so you are spot on. The energy economics and energy politics play into this. And I think it is the right thing to do.

Mr. POE. I agree with you. Amen.

Mr. ROHRABACHER. Thank you very much.

Mr. DUNCAN. I yield back.

Mr. ROHRABACHER. Now I would like to turn to Brad Sherman.

Mr. SHERMAN. I have a question, but it would also apply to some of my colleagues from gas- and oil-producing States. But I will direct it to Mr. Brzezinski.

Okay. We pay about $4 or $5 a unit for natural gas here. They pay $10 in Europe. And liquefied natural gas is sold in Asia for $15. I don't know if any of my colleagues from oil-producing States can explain which companies headquartered in their districts want to sell the gas for $10 in Europe and forgo the $15 they can get in Asia.

But the question for the witness is, do you sense that the American taxpayer, or the German taxpayer, or the German consumer wants to pay that additional $5?

Mr. BRZEZINSKI. For gas from the United States, sir?

Mr. SHERMAN. Yes.

Mr. BRZEZINSKI. Probably not. But my sense is that LNG exports by the United States would be uninhibited, would probably flow mostly to Asia. There is no question about that. But the LNG market is increasingly globalized. That flow of U.S. LNG into Asia pushes excess, other LNG from other sources, over to Europe. And, in fact, it has already been the case to a certain degree.

Mr. SHERMAN. Again, the world price is $15 for liquefied natural gas. It is $10 for Russian piped natural gas. Who is going to pay the extra $5?

Mr. BRZEZINSKI. They will always go to the cheaper gas. But the benefits, the geopolitical benefits, geoeconomic benefits of uninhibited U.S.——

Mr. SHERMAN. Who pays? Are the Germans lining up to say, damn it, we want to pay Japanese prices rather than Russian prices, to pay the same price as Japan for liquefied natural gas? They could get liquefied natural gas from Qatar and other Arab states and they don't take a single cubic foot of it because it costs 50 percent more than the Russian natural gas.

So if the German Government and the German people don't want to pay the extra money, are you suggesting that the United States taxpayer pay the difference?

Mr. BRZEZINSKI. No.

Mr. SHERMAN. Okay.

Let me go on to another series of questions. Okay.

Rebels had SA–11s or similar technology. They shot down the plane. They thought they were shooting down a Ukrainian plane. It seems to be viewed as almost cut and dry that they must have gotten the SA–11s as a gift from Moscow. But much of their other weaponry they have seized on the battlefield or just kind of walked into at military bases and taken equipment owned by the Ukrainian Government.

So did the Ukrainian Government have SA–11s or similar technology capable of, even if it had to be a lucky shot, but capable of perhaps hitting a plane at 33,000 square feet? Does the Ukraine have that technology? Mr. Taylor?

Ambassador TAYLOR. Certainly, they have that technology. But they were nowhere near the area.

Mr. SHERMAN. No. Well, are we certain that none of that technology fell into rebel hands at any time during this conflict, including knowing that the prior government of the Ukraine was pro-Russian and had most of its support on the same areas where the separatists enjoy support?

Ambassador TAYLOR. Mr. Sherman, I think it is very clear that the separatists fired the weapon.

Mr. SHERMAN. That is not my question.

Ambassador TAYLOR. Where it came from is your question. And I don't think we know precisely which piece actually came from the Ukrainians.

Mr. SHERMAN. But are you certain that not a——

Ambassador TAYLOR. What we have seen has come across the border.

Mr. SHERMAN. Some came across the border. Were others taken from the Ukrainian Government? Do we have a full accounting from the Ukrainian Government, hey, at separation of the Soviet Union, we had so many SA–11 systems, we acquired so many systems, we can account for all of those systems? Or are we just kind of taking it out of anger that you have these systems both in the Ukraine and in Russia, and it must have been the Russian systems that the separatists got their hand on?

Mr. Salvia.

Mr. SALVIA. I am afraid I just don't know the answer to that. Sorry.

Mr. SHERMAN. Okay. My time has expired. Thank you.

Mr. ROHRABACHER. Well, I want to thank our witnesses today. What we will have now is just a summary from the chairmen and ranking members of the committees of jurisdiction. And we will start with Judge Poe.

Mr. POE. I thank the chairman.

Thanks again, gentlemen, for being here.

It just seems to me that this whole operation in Ukraine and other places is driven by Putin. He is doing it, as you have stated, to help himself politically back home. It does sell. It does raise the Russian flag at home. And his quest for aggression—aggression, I think that is the best way to call this activity—he wants influence back in areas that belonged to the Soviet Union. But his motive goes back further. I think it goes back to the days of the czar. That is the way I see this.

The U.S., West response has been weak, and it is shown because it hasn't stopped the aggression. The United States, along with the West, freedom-loving folks, need to impose sanctions that actually work. And we also should, I think, help the Ukrainians defend their own country.

I do believe that we should open up markets and give Western Europe, Eastern Europe alternatives to natural gas. In answer to the ranking member's question, yes, there is a specific company in Houston, Texas, Accelerated Energy, that wants to sell natural gas to the Ukrainians and will be able to do that within a year if they could get permission to do so.

We are flaring off natural gas in Texas and in the Dakotas to the amount of 1 million homes losing energy because we have so much natural gas. It is a world market. But they want the opportunity to sell more natural gas on the world market. But I think that it is part of the long-range strategy to buttress the aggression, not just with helping Ukraine militarily, but helping alternatives economically, including those economic.

Putin has not been stopped. I don't know that he will be stopped unless we actually want some answers and some results from the aggression. I think his plan is long term. But opportunities, when they arise, he will take advantage of those. So that is the way I see it.

I will yield back to the chairman of the European Committee.

Mr. ROHRABACHER. Thank you very much.

And, Mr. Sherman, do you have a summary that you would like to offer?

Mr. SHERMAN. As to the export of natural gas, the major reason, the major obstacle is the enormous economic cost of liquefying, transporting, and then regasifying the gas. There is a lot of natural gas in the Arab world. The Arabs will sell it for the highest price. They are driven by the exact same capitalist calculations as American oil companies. They sell it all to Asia and none to Europe.

As to the fact that you need permission to export natural gas, you don't need permission to export it to any country that has a free trade treatment with the United States, including South Korea. And in addition, the administration has licensed some export projects as being in the interests of the United States.

I do not think that those who liquefy natural gas want to charge less than $15 a unit for it. And I don't think there is anybody in

Europe, EU or otherwise, that wants to pay more than the Russian price, which is basically $10.

Looking at the Middle East as an analogy, we are urging Maliki to make the best possible offer to the Sunnis, even though you could probably argue that 51 percent of the Iraqi people would, if they had their druthers, give the Sunnis nothing.

We need to urge Kiev to make the best possible offer to those who want autonomy. And that includes protection of the Russian language, that includes electing the governors of the oblasts, that includes local budgetary control, it includes the other elements that are part of the reasonable, nonseparatist political parties that are seeking autonomy for the various regions. And it is not enough to make vague statements, we need specifics.

And I yield back.

Mr. ROHRABACHER. And Mr. Keating.

Mr. KEATING. Mr. Chairman, I think it is clear that this hearing has made a couple of major points, one of them being that this issue is not discrete to Ukraine. This is indeed an issue of high prominence to all of Europe in the future, and that includes efforts to establish rule of law, that includes efforts for economic growth and democracy.

And it is also clear, I think, that much of Russia's aggression isn't quite as strategic in a long-term sense as it is reactionary. And one of the things that bears watching is what signals the European countries and the U.S. are giving back, because I think that will determine what actions Russia takes in the future as well.

And along those lines, I think we also understand the importance of our economic progress together. And by that, even though it wasn't mentioned today, I look at enhancement of the TTIP agreement, the free trade agreement with Europe as a very important object that we should continue to work forward with, because it is within that economic strength that we will be able to stabilize and move Europe forward. And that is our best way of countering these kind of senseless acts of aggression.

Yield back, Mr. Chairman.

Mr. ROHRABACHER. Well, thank you very much.

Well, I think this was a very worthwhile hearing. I am sorry that we didn't actually get more specific suggestions, although I think that we have looked, taken a look at the situation a little closer than has been looked at in the last month or two as this crisis seems to be getting worse and worse.

Let me just note, historically I have spent most of my life fighting communism and fighting the Soviet Union. And let me just note, same is true of Mr. Salvia, who was the executive assistant to the president for Radio Free Europe and Radio Liberty between 1988 and 1993.

I always think it is best to go specifically at the issues at hand, but people do have a right, and the ranking member certainly has a right to question the validity of witnesses. But I found you a very credible witness, and know of your background and the things you have done to help defeat communism during my time with the Reagan administration and before and after.

Let me note that there seem to be some people in the United States who are hellbent to reignite the Cold War. I mean, they feel more comfortable with trying to go at Russia. After the Soviet Union fell, there was a tremendous potential to making Russia our friend. A tremendous potential. They withdrew their troops from Eastern Europe, the Russians were open to all kinds of interacting and becoming part of the world community. And a tremendous opportunity was squandered.

Over the years there have been people, and I believe that, unfortunately, it has a lot to do with the political forces in our country that were pandering to the people who had a grudge against Russia. And I am talking about there is obviously a justified grudge that the people of Eastern Europe have had against Russia because under communism Russia committed so many crimes against those people, whether it be the Poles, the Czechs, the Bulgarians, or the Ukrainians in particular. We know the millions of people who lost their lives during the 1900s because the Russians came in with their communism, and millions of people died horrible deaths, Ukrainian people. And so we understand that there is a grudge out there blaming the Russian people for communism. That is understandable.

But our job when the Soviet Union collapsed and people turned to become Russia, a democratic Russia, I think it was our job to try to not pay attention to those grudge and pander to those people who wanted to get even, but instead to try to build a new world.

And I don't think we did. I think we decided that there would be allies made politically, locally, where my Polish friends, my Ukrainian friends who can't understand why I would want to make peace with Russia now, even after I spent my whole life fighting them.

I think we lost a great opportunity there. And maybe it is not lost. But we have turned what was a potentially good friend into an adversary. And there is no other way to look at Russia now. They are an adversary. And what I am afraid of is now we are going to turn an adversary into an enemy, and we don't want that. I don't want that. I hope the American people, I don't think they do either.

I would hope that the testimony at the hearing today has at least motivated some people to reach out to each other. I would hope that the points about making the best possible offer by the Government of Ukraine, should be making the best possible offer to the separatists to try to find a way to end that violence, and that we should be supporting that type of positive move.

And I would hope that after this hearing today that we try to take a look at what is going on with honesty and with a goal of creating a more peaceful region of that part of the world and thus a more peaceful world, rather than a belligerent approach to this, what is going on, that will end up creating a wholesale enemy out of the Russian people when right now we can possibly work with them to create some peace and offer some honest working together and cooperation toward that goal.

So with that said, I want to thank the witnesses. Thank you all very much. And thank my ranking member for a spirited, a very spirited time period here. Thank you all. And this hearing is now adjourned.

[Whereupon, at 12:16 p.m., the subcommittees were adjourned.]

APPENDIX

MATERIAL SUBMITTED FOR THE RECORD

JOINT SUBCOMMITTEE HEARING NOTICE
COMMITTEE ON FOREIGN AFFAIRS
U.S. HOUSE OF REPRESENTATIVES
WASHINGTON, DC 20515-6128

Subcommittee on Europe, Eurasia, and Emerging Threats
Dana Rohrabacher (R-CA), Chairman

Subcommittee on Terrorism, Nonproliferation, and Trade
Ted Poe (R-TX), Chairman

July 25, 2014

TO: MEMBERS OF THE COMMITTEE ON FOREIGN AFFAIRS

You are respectfully requested to attend an OPEN hearing of the Committee on Foreign Affairs, to be held jointly by the Subcommittee on Europe, Eurasia, and Emerging Threats and the Subcommittee on Terrorism, Nonproliferation, and Trade in Room 2172 of the Rayburn House Office Building (and available live on the Committee website at http://www.ForeignAffairs.house.gov):

DATE: Tuesday, July 29, 2014

TIME: 10:15 a.m.

SUBJECT: The Shootdown of Malaysian Flight 17 and the Escalating Crisis in Ukraine

WITNESSES: Mr. Ian Brzezinski
Resident Senior Fellow
Brent Scowcroft Center on International Security
Atlantic Council

Mr. Anthony Salvia
Executive Director
American Institute in Ukraine

The Honorable William B. Taylor
Vice President for Middle East and Africa
United States Institute of Peace
(Former United States Ambassador to Ukraine)

Leon Aron, Ph.D.
Resident Scholar and Director of Russian Studies
The American Enterprise Institute

By Direction of the Chairman

COMMITTEE ON FOREIGN AFFAIRS

MINUTES OF SUBCOMMITTEE ON _____*Europe, Eurasia and Emerging Threats joint with Subcommittee on Terrorism, Nonproliferation, and Trade*_____ HEARING

Day____*Tuesday*____Date_____*July 29, 2014*____Room_____*2172*_____

Starting Time ____*10:13am*____ Ending Time ____*1:15pm*____

Recesses |____| (____to ____) (____to ____) (____to ____) (____to ____) (____to ____) (____to ____)

Presiding Member(s)

Rep. Rohrabacher & Rep. Poe

Check all of the following that apply:

Open Session ☐   Electronically Recorded (taped) ☑
Executive (closed) Session ☐   Stenographic Record ☐
Televised ☐

TITLE OF HEARING:

The Shootdown of Malaysian Flight 17 and the Escalating Crisis in Ukraine

SUBCOMMITTEE MEMBERS PRESENT:

Rep. Poe, Rep. Duncan, Rep. Cotton, Rep. Perry, Rep. Brooks

NON-SUBCOMMITTEE MEMBERS PRESENT: *(Mark with an * if they are not members of full committee.)*

Rep. Royce

HEARING WITNESSES: Same as meeting notice attached? Yes ☑ No ☐
(If "no", please list below and include title, agency, department, or organization.)

STATEMENTS FOR THE RECORD: *(List any statements submitted for the record.)*

Rep. Keating

TIME SCHEDULED TO RECONVENE _____
or
TIME ADJOURNED ____*1:15pm*____

Subcommittee Staff Director

MATERIAL SUBMITTED FOR THE RECORD BY THE HONORABLE WILLIAM KEATING, A
REPRESENTATIVE IN CONGRESS FROM THE COMMONWEALTH OF MASSACHUSETTS

Sympathy for the Devils

Inside the shadowy Washington PR network with ties to dictators' cronies, war criminals, and suspicious Ukrainian arms transporters.

BY MICHAEL WEISS

R ussia's annexation of Crimea and its creeping invasion of southern and eastern Ukraine have had a small but discernible impact on the tenebrous world of Washington public relations. Yesterday's plausibly defensible "partner" in the Kremlin has become today's revanchist bully, intent on an *Anschluss* of sovereign European territory. As a result, those who have worked quietly over the past few years to enhance the image and credibility of the Kremlin, its former allies, its client states, or its commercial associates now find themselves on the receiving end of greater scrutiny -- and of the more emboldened legal countermeasures of nongovernmental organizations whose efforts to uncover or investigate these unflattering associations have been previously hampered by the constant threat of civil litigation.

The nice thing about a foreign-policy crisis is that it can make the U.S. government an accidental safeguard against libel. On April 11, C4ADS, originally founded as the Center for Advanced Defense Studies, a Washington-based global conflict and security research group, filed a complaint requesting a declaratory judgment and anti-suit injunction in the Superior Court of the District of Columbia against three defendants who now suddenly find themselves in unfashionable company. The first is Kaalbye Shipping International, a Ukrainian shipping company registered in the British Virgin Islands but based in the largely Russian-controlled Ukrainian port city of Odessa. C4ADS maintains in its 2013 report, "The Odessa Network: Mapping Facilitators of Russian and Ukrainian Arms Transfers," a copy of which is attached to its court complaint, that Kaalbye transported Russian military equipment to Syria, China, Venezuela, and Angola and that the company's senior personnel have close ties to "organs of state power" in Moscow. Kaalbye, C4ADS also says, has shipped materiel to rogue regimes from St. Petersburg and the southeastern Ukrainian port city of Oktyabrsk. C4ADS calls Kaalbye in that report "the single most active shipper of Russian and Ukrainian weapons."

The second defendant is Kaalbye's Washington-based public relations firm, Global Strategic Communications Group (GSCG), which "has published articles on behalf of KAALBYE that defame C4ADS," according to the court filing.

The third defendant is Peter Hannaford, GSCG's senior consultant, who is one of the alleged defamers. Hannaford published two attacks on the NGO and concurrent defenses of Kaalbye in the conservative outlets the *American Spectator* and the *Washington Times*. Neither of those publications disclosed his affiliation with a paid agent of the shipping company.

Kaalbye's own legal counsel is another, albeit more prominent, Washington presence: international law and lobbying firm Patton Boggs, which has apparently asked C4ADS to "repudiate" what Kaalbye alleges are "libelous statements" made in "The Odessa Network." For its part, C4ADS counters that the statements are not only accurate but are consistent with numerous press reports, Kaalbye's own admissions, and even U.S. military statements about the shipping company's activities and assets. C4ADS's case "arises from KAALBYE's serious and immediate threats of litigation against C4ADS, and from KAALBYE, GSCG's and HANNAFORD's defamation statements and tortious interference with C4ADS's business relations," the court filing states. Farley Mesko, one of the two authors of "The Odessa Network" and the chief operating officer of C4ADS, told

58

Foreign Policy: "As we see it, this was a matter of sue or be sued. Offense or defense. Given the groundless nature of Kaalbye's complaints and their efforts to defame our professional reputation, we prefer offense."

And C4ADS certainly goes out of its way to give it. The most intriguing reading in its filing concerns GSCG, a relatively obscure PR outfit, the website of which is now offline. GSCG's senior staff consist of a handful of Beltway insiders with histories of publicly defending or contractually working on behalf of odious international figures, many of whom are now sanctioned by the U.S. government.

To begin with, GSCG has acted in the past as the legally registered foreign agent, under the U.S. Foreign Agents Registration Act (FARA), of the "leadership of the Rodina Party," which included its then-chairman Dmitry Rogozin, now the sharp-tongued Russian deputy prime minister in charge of Russia's growing defense industry and the chairman of its Military Industrial Commission. Historian Timothy Snyder has described Rodina, which means "Motherland" in Russian, as a "far-right" party. "In 2005 some of its deputies signed a petition to the Russian prosecutor general asking that all Jewish organizations be banned from Russia," Snyder wrote in a recent essay for the *New York Review of Books*. Also, in 2005, Rodina was banned from taking part in the Duma elections after complaints that its advertisements incited race hatred. Rogozin became Russia's ambassador to NATO in 2008, from which position he strongly opposed Ukraine's and Georgia's accession to the military alliance. In March of this year, the Obama administration added Rogozin to its sanctions list on a host of Russian officials and politically connected oligarchs for his role in Russian President Vladimir Putin's invasion and annexation of Crimea. Rogozin, a friend of Putin's favorite action hero, Steven Seagal, laughed off his inclusion, tweeting: "Comrade

@BarackObama, what should do those who have neither accounts nor property abroad? Or U didn't think about it?" According to GSCG's FARA declaration, in 2005 GSCG was Rogozin's public relations arm in the United States, responsible for "preparing or disseminating informational materials" and representing him across all media platforms. The PR firm received more than $30,000 for its services.

FP contacted GSCG's current managing partner, Darren Spinck, for comment about this work for Rogozin and Rodina. GSCG's attorney responded: "GSCG has not rendered any services for Rodina since early 2006."

Hannaford, meanwhile, resigned a decade ago as managing director of the Committee on the Present Danger, a day after the former anti-Soviet advisory body was relaunched to help prosecute the war on terror. Why? The *New York Sun* disclosed that Hannaford's former lobbying firm, Carmen Group, had charged $40,000 a year to act as the U.S. representative of the far-right Austrian Freedom Party, then headed by the now-deceased Jörg Haider, who once praised the Third Reich for its "orderly employment policy" and paid a "solidarity visit" to Saddam Hussein in Baghdad in 2002. (In fairness, the solidarity may have been slightly incentivized; an investigation carried out by the Austrian newsmagazine *Profil* in 2010 suggested that Haider was paid over $1 million by the Iraqi dictator.) Hannaford defended his work for the Freedom Party, saying at the time that while Haider "said many silly things and he was trying to live them down," other Austrian MPs from the party were "quite levelheaded" and supported "sensible" programs. Nevertheless, Hannaford seems to have regained a level of prominence in the Committee on the Present Danger in the ensuing years. The group's website, which appears to have been updated as recently as March of this year,

60

now informs us that he is not only still a member but was recently elected vice president of its board.

FP attempted to reach Hannaford for comment via both his Committee and personal email addresses (the second of which was listed on his *American Spectator* biography but appears to be no longer valid), as well as through GSCG's listed phone number. These attempts were unsuccessful. FP also tried to relay our request for comment from Hannaford through Spinck, but Hannaford did not reply to this request.

Odd Friends Indeed

Judging by their open-source paper trails, GSCG's executives seem to have a fondness for a wide assortment of autocrats and strongmen. In 2003, James George Jatras, now the managing director of GSCG, worked for the Washington-based law firm Venable, which signed a lobbying agreement with Alex Kiselev, the representative of then-Prime Minister Viktor Yanukovych. This agreement, a copy of which was originally published by the Ukrainian newspaper *Ukrainska Pravda* in 2009, was witnessed and signed by Spinck. It stipulated that "Venable will work to ensure access to high-level figures in the Executive and Legislative Branches of government, media, think tanks, and other entities that may be useful to enhancement of Mr. Yanukovych's profile in the United States." Venable would also, so states the agreement, "write and distribute talking points, press advisories, and other materials favorable to Mr. Yanukovych to influential figures in the United States, particularly in Washington, D.C., to the end of stimulating positive media coverage and policy analysis in the United States of Mr. Yanukovych and the value to the United States of working with him for better ties between Washington and Kyiv." An addendum to the agreement also held that Venable would "endeavor to arrange a personal meeting at the White House between Prime Minister Yanukovych and President Bush, under circumstances appropriate for a visiting head of government." The retainer for trying to make this meeting happen was $20,000; the "success fee" was $60,000.

When contacted by FP, Jatras, the former Venable employee who signed the agreement with Kiselev, declined to answer questions regarding his own view of Yanukovych's handling of the Euromaidan protests, the Ukrainian president's subsequent removal from power, or whether -- if there were no U.S. sanctions currently in place against Yanukovych -- Jatras would represent him again today.

The reason that *Ukrainska Pravda* bothered to uncover this intimate arrangement between American "PR-niki" and the Yanukovych regime was that one of the newspaper's journalists, Serhiy Leshchenko, had been invited to participate in an event put on by a Kiev-based organization known as the American Institute in Ukraine. The person who did the inviting was Dmytro Dzhanhirov, the director of 1+1, a Ukrainian state television channel, which had made a special project of vilifying the Orange Revolution leader and eventual Ukrainian president Viktor Yushchenko in 2004. Dzhanhirov claimed to be "assisting" the newish institute. But the more Leshchenko looked into the outfit, the less impressed he was. "Usually the American Institute in Ukraine," he wrote, "uses an outdated format: holding a round table and inviting a speaker from the U.S., who is meant to convince those present of the mistake of Ukraine's path into NATO."

As of the time of this article's publication, the American Institute in Ukraine lists as its communications manager GSCG founder Darren Spinck, and as its executive director Anthony Salvia, another director of GSCG. However, the Ukrainian phone number listed for the American Institute is out of service. Spinck's attorney told

FP that this organization "has not conducted activities inside Ukraine since violence erupted in Kiev and has closed its office there."

According to his bio at the now-offline GSCG website, Salvia served in a variety of roles in Ronald Reagan's administration, including as the Pentagon's staff assistant in the Office of European and NATO Affairs, a position that seems to have turned him off to expanding the alliance into countries of the former Soviet Union. He also lists himself as an "[o]fficial observer to the Russian presidential election 2012 ... and the Russian parliamentary election 2011," but doesn't disclose what his observations were of those two exercises in so-called "managed democracy."

Not that Salvia is shy about his tendency in Ukraine's domestic politics. He wrote an op-ed for the *Kyiv Post* in January 2011 recommending Yanukovych -- then only a year into his abortive presidency -- for the Nobel Peace Prize. "One of [Yanukovych's] first actions was to cut a deal with Russia on natural gas transit to Europe, in exchange for price concessions for Ukraine's consumption," Salvia wrote. "He followed that up with dropping permanently the previous regime's efforts to drag Ukraine into NATO even in the face of overwhelming popular opposition (so much for Orange Revolution-styled democracy), and opting for non-aligned status instead." In that op-ed, Salvia also derided the accusation that Yanukovych was Putin's "puppet" -- an assessment that may be worth revisiting now that the ex-president, fresh from overseeing the murder of a hundred people in Kiev (with the ample aid of Russian intelligence agents) and fresh from being sanctioned by both the United States and the European Union for these crimes, fled Ukraine and alighted in the decidedly aligned environs of Moscow and Rostov-on-Don. "Judging by results, by tangible contributions to peace,

Yanukovych's achievements in a short period of time are impressive," the op-ed concluded. "It is reasonable to suggest that he be counted among the [Peace Prize] nominees." (FP tried unsuccessfully through Spinck and the now apparently defunct American Institute in Ukraine to reach Salvia for comment.)

> **Even accused war criminals have received a helping hand from GSCG brass.**

Even accused war criminals have received a helping hand from GSCG brass. In 2004, Jatras, previously a senior foreign-policy analyst at the Senate Republican Policy Committee, gave testimony in defense of Slobodan Milosevic during the latter's tribunal at The Hague, based on what he himself acknowledged was no "actual, direct evidence coming from the [the Balkans]," but rather from evidence "solely ... within the government and the thinking in the government in Washington." Jatras testified, *inter alia*, that Bill Clinton's administration was complicit in Iran's delivery of arms to Bosnian Muslims via the Croatian government -- at a time when the United Nations had imposed an arms embargo on the former Yugoslavia -- and that it had ignored, as he recalled in court, the "al Qaeda and the Islamist orientation of the [Alija] Izetbegovic government" in Sarajevo. He also believed, as he stated at The Hague, that the Clinton White House "had made a decision to intervene militarily in Kosovo, either by creating circumstances where Serbia would consent to an occupation of Kosovo or through undertaking military action to bring about that result." Some of Jatras's testimony was based on Senate Republican Policy Committee reports he had authored in the late 1990s on the Balkan conflicts, and some was based on a House select subcommittee report on the possible U.S. role in Iranian arms transfers to Bosnia and Croatia, which carried majority and minority dissenting opinions, divided along partisan lines.

The full article can be accessed online on Foreign Policy:
http://www.foreignpolicy.com/articles/2014/05/21/sympathy_for_the_devils_gscg_kaalbye_c4ads_odessa_network

www.ingramcontent.com/pod-product-compliance
Lightning Source LLC
Chambersburg PA
CBHW081243280526

45787CB00006B/2775